1st Workshop on AI and Scientific Discovery (AISD): Directions and Opportunities

Albuquerque, New Mexico, USA
3 May 2025

ISBN: 979-8-3313-1909-0

Printed from e-media with permission by:

Curran Associates, Inc.
57 Morehouse Lane
Red Hook, NY 12571

Some format issues inherent in the e-media version may also appear in this print version.

Association for Computational Linguistics
209 N. Eighth Street
Stroudsburg, Pennsylvania 18360

Phone: 1-570-476-8006
Fax: 1-570-476-0860

acl@aclweb.org

Additional copies of this publication are available from:

Curran Associates, Inc.
57 Morehouse Lane
Red Hook, NY 12571 USA
Phone: 845-758-0400
Fax: 845-758-2633
Email: curran@proceedings.com
Web: www.proceedings.com

AISD 2025

Annual Conference of the Nations of the Americas Chapter of the Association for Computational Linguistics

Proceedings of the 1st Workshop on AI and Scientific Discovery (AISD): Directions and Opportunities

May 3, 2025

The AISD organizers gratefully acknowledge the support from the following sponsors.

Gold

Ai2

Order copies of this and other ACL proceedings from:

Association for Computational Linguistics (ACL)
317 Sidney Baker St. S
Suite 400 - 134
Kerrville, TX 78028
USA
Tel: +1-855-225-1962
acl@aclweb.org

Introduction

Welcome to AISD, the First Workshop on AI & Scientific Discovery, co-located with NAACL 2025 in Albuquerque, New Mexico.

Just as coding assistants have dramatically increased productivity for coding tasks over the last two years, researchers in the NLP community have begun to explore methods and opportunities ahead for creating scientific assistants that can help with the process of scientific discovery and increase the pace at which novel discoveries are made. Over the last year, language models have been used to create problem-general scientific discovery assistants that are not restricted to narrow problem domains or formulations. Such applications hold opportunities for assisting researchers in broad domains, or scientific reasoning more generally. Beyond assisting, a growing body of work has begun to focus on the prospect of creating largely autonomous scientific discovery agents that can make novel discoveries with minimal human intervention. These recent developments highlight the possibility of rapidly accelerating the pace of scientific discovery in the near term. Given the influx of researchers into this expanding field, this workshop proposes to serve as a vehicle for bringing together a diverse set of perspectives from this quickly expanding subfield, helping to disseminate the latest results, standardize evaluation, foster collaboration between groups, and allow discussing aspirational goals for 2025 and beyond. This workshop welcomes and covers a wide range of topics, including (but not limited to): Literature-based Discovery, Agent-centered Approaches, Automated Experiment Execution, Automated Replication, Data-driven Discovery, Discovery in Virtual Environments, Discovery with Humans in the Loop, and Assistants for Scientific Writing.

A total of 7 papers appear in the proceedings. 24 papers were presented at the workshop itself, with the rest being submitted under two archival options: cross-submissions (Findings papers or those already presented at other venues, such as ICLR, EMNLP, NeurIPS, or the NAACL main conference), and regular non-archival submissions (unpublished work). The latter went through a normal peer review process. These papers can be found on the AISD website: https://ai-and-scientific-discovery.github.io/

Six papers were featured as oral presentations. These papers represented a selection of strong work that the organizers felt would be of broad interest to workshop participants. In addition, we featured four invited talks: Heng Ji, Jure Leskovec, Peter Clark, and Marinka Zitniki. We are thankful to all reviewers for their help in the selection of the program, for their readiness to engage in thoughtful discussions about individual papers, and for providing valuable feedback to the authors. We would also like to thank the NAACL workshop organizers for all the valuable help and support with the organizational aspects of the conference. Finally, we would like to thank all our authors and presenters for making this such an exciting event!

Peter Jansen, Bhavana Dalvi Mishra, Harsh Trivedi, Bodhisattwa Prasad Majumder, Tom Hope, Tushar Khot, Doug Downey, Eric Horvitz
AISD organizers

Organizing Committee

Organizers

Bhavana Dalvi Mishra, Allen Institute for Artificial Intelligence
Doug Downey, Allen Institute for Artificial Intelligence
Tom Hope, Allen Institute for Artificial Intelligence / Hebrew University of Jerusalem
Eric Horvitz, Microsoft
Peter Jansen, University of Arizona / Allen Institute for Artificial Intelligence
Tushar Khot, Google DeepMind
Bodhisattwa Prasad Majumder, Allen Institute for Artificial Intelligence
Harsh Trivedi, Allen Institute for Artificial Intelligence

Program Committee

Program Chairs

Bhavana Dalvi Mishra, Allen Institute for Artificial Intelligence
Doug Downey, Allen Institute for Artificial Intelligence
Tom Hope, Allen Institute for Artificial Intelligence and Hebrew University of Jerusalem
Eric Horvitz, Microsoft
Peter Jansen, University of Arizona and Allen Institute for Artificial Intelligence
Tushar Khot, Google DeepMind
Bodhisattwa Prasad Majumder, Allen Institute for Artificial Intelligence
Harsh Trivedi, Allen Institute for Artificial Intelligence

Reviewers

Jinheon Baek, Chandrayee Basu

Srinivasarao Daruna

Shivanshu Gupta

Naoya Inoue

Uri Katz

Arun Balajiee Lekshmi Narayanan, Daniel J. Liebling

Enrique Noriega-Atala

Zayne Rea Sprague

Rosni Vasu

Table of Contents

Variable Extraction for Model Recovery in Scientific Literature

Chunwei Liu[1], Enrique Noriega[2],
Adarsh Pyarelal[2], Clayton T. Morrison[2], Michael Cafarella[1]
[1]MIT CSAIL [2]The University of Arizona
{chunwei, michjc}@csail.mit.edu
{enoriega, adarsh, claytonm}@arizona.edu

Abstract

Due to the increasing productivity in the scientific community, it is difficult to keep up with the literature without the assistance of AI methods. This paper evaluates various methods for extracting mathematical model variables from epidemiological studies, such as "infection rate (α)," "recovery rate (γ)," and "mortality rate (μ)." Variable extraction appears to be a basic task, but plays a pivotal role in recovering models from scientific literature. Once extracted, we can use these variables for automatic mathematical modeling, simulation, and replication of published results. We also introduce a benchmark dataset comprising manually-annotated variable descriptions and variable values extracted from scientific papers. Our analysis shows that LLM-based solutions perform the best. Despite the incremental benefits of combining rule-based extraction outputs with LLMs, the leap in performance attributed to the transfer-learning and instruction-tuning capabilities of LLMs themselves is far more significant. This investigation demonstrates the potential of LLMs to enhance automatic comprehension of scientific artifacts and for automatic model recovery and simulation.

1 Introduction

The surge in scientific publications, now exceeding five million articles annually [1], represents a challenge for any individual or group seeking to comprehensively review the state of the art of any given discipline. The sheer size of the information warrants the use of automated information extraction technologies to sort through and navigate vast scientific corpora. In this work, we study the scientific literature that concerns mathematical modeling, in order to aid model recovery (Pyarelal et al., 2020; Sharp et al., 2019; Schaffhauser et al., 2023): the creation of symbolic representations of mathematical models through information extraction methods applied to the scientific literature[2].

> $1+\alpha R$ can be thought of as $S+I+R+\alpha R$. Given that $S+I+R=1$, this is equivalent to the term $1+\alpha R$. Figure 1 illustrates shield immunity impacts on a SIR epidemic with $R_0 = 2.5$ (R_0 is the basic reproduction number). In this SIR model, shield immunity reduces the epidemic peak and shortens the duration of epidemic spread. Shielding in this context acts as a negative feedback loop, given that the effective reproduction number is given by $\mathcal{R}_{\text{eff}}(t)/\mathcal{R}_0 = S(t)/(1+\alpha R(t))$. As a result, interaction substitution increases as recovered individuals increase in number and are identified. For example, in the case of $\alpha = 20$, the epidemic con-

Text Span		Variable Extraction		
Start	End	Name	Description	Value
185	193	R0	-	2.5
195	232	R0	Basic reproduction number	-
634	640	α	-	20

Figure 1: Example of variable extraction from a scientific paper text, illustrating the process of identifying and extracting elements such as the variable name, description, and initial value into a structured format. The figure highlights different types of extraction: variable description pairs in light orange and variable value pairs in light purple.

We introduce the task of *variable extraction*: the identification and organization elements such as variable names, descriptions, and initial values into a structured format, as illustrated in Figure 1. Variable extraction is a crucial step toward model recovery as it unlocks the basic units of models presented in scientific papers. By doing so, it not only deepens the understanding of the research but also facilitates the further rebuilding and enhancement of these models.

The complexity of variable extraction arises from the diverse forms and locations in which variables can appear within a document. Variables may be embedded in text, figures, tables, or even scattered throughout the paper as single characters, multiple words, single values, or ranges. This variability, coupled with their interdependencies,

[1]`https://wordsrated.com/number-of-academic-papers-published-per-year/`

[2]https://www.darpa.mil/research/programs/automating-scientific-knowledge-extraction-modeling

Proceedings of the 1st Workshop on AI and Scientific Discovery: Directions and Opportunities, pages 1–12
May 3, 2025

underscores the importance and challenge of this task. Effective variable extraction is essential for identifying errors in models and converting them into executable code, which improves the accuracy and practicality of scientific research.

Until recently, the extraction of model variables from texts commonly employed conventional machine learning methods such as named-entity recognition (Tjong Kim Sang and De Meulder, 2003) and relation extraction (Zhang et al., 2017). However, the emergence of Large Language Models (LLMs) (Touvron et al., 2023; Jiang et al., 2023; OpenAI, 2024) has marked a significant change. With their enhanced natural language processing (NLP) capabilities, LLMs provide new options to enhance the efficiency and effectiveness of scientific text analysis, particularly in the extraction of variables and the broader process of model recovery.

To investigate the potential of these methods, we annotated 22 scientific papers, creating a public information extraction benchmark. This benchmark is designed to facilitate the evaluation of various variable extraction techniques. Subsequently, We then conduct a comprehensive evaluation of several LLMs designed for the variable extraction task, alongside a rule-based method and an optimized AI pipeline framework to provide additional perspective.

Our evaluation indicated that although no existing solution excels in the variable extraction task, certain configurations could significantly improve the extraction quality. The best-performing baseline model achieved an F1 score of only 0.49 or 0.60, depending on the evaluation metric used. However, by integrating rule-based approaches with LLMs, we enhanced performance, achieving F1 scores of up to 0.53 and 0.64, respectively. This integration highlights the complementary strengths of different methodologies: rule-based approaches provide additional variable extraction options from a different perspective, thus improving the performance of LLM. Overall, LLM-based solutions outperformed conventional rule-based solutions, demonstrating their capability to enhance the automatic comprehension of scientific artifacts and establish a robust foundation for automatic model recovery and simulation. These insights contribute to the ongoing discourse on improving the understanding and utilization of scientific literature, paving the way for more efficient and accurate scientific research in the era of information overload.

2 Related Work

In this work we focus on the intake of scientific literature to identify and recover the elements of mathematical models: *variable descriptions* and *variable values*, as described in text and we rely on NLP methods to recover them.

The field of Information Extraction (IE) is one of the main applications of NLP. It consists on identifying and extracting structured information from human-written text. These structure data, consists of named-entity recognition (Tjong Kim Sang and De Meulder, 2003) and relation extraction (Zhang et al., 2017). The structured data is then leveraged by downstream applications such as building knowledge bases (Shimorina et al., 2022), slot-filling (Chen et al., 2019), visualization for interactions (Noriega-Atala et al., 2023), or performing downstream inference (Lao et al., 2011).

Large language models (Touvron et al., 2023; Jiang et al., 2023; OpenAI, 2024), with their increasing versatility have become a useful tool for information extraction (Xu et al., 2024). Building on traditional models and LLMs, numerous systems have been proposed to automatically optimize AI-powered analytics and information extraction according to user preferences (Zheng et al., 2023; Chen et al., 2023; Liu et al., 2024; Patel et al., 2024; Lin et al., 2024; Liu et al., 2025). This work takes inspiration from these methods to identify and extract variable information.

Due to its sheer size, scientific literature is frequently the subject of IE research. Some disciplines, such as health sciences and biomedical research, have received a lot of attention due to their high potential for impact. Because of this, there exists a solid record of research activity around that has produced multiple high-quality datasets (Mohan and Li, 2019; Kim et al., 2013; Ohta et al., 2013; Saier et al., 2024) and systems (Valenzuela-Escárcega et al., 2018; Neumann et al., 2019; Wang et al., 2018) focused on clinical and medical applications.

Prior work at extracting mathematical elements has used various classical NLP methods. A CRF model to align mathematical expressions with their definitions (Yoko et al., 2012); a pattern-based data mining method to build mathematical ontologies from LaTeXsources (Jeschke et al., 2007); a NER system for abstract mathematical concepts (Collard et al., 2022) extracting mathematical elements from scientific text. Our work builds upon the ideas from prior research and introduces a high-quality, manually curated dataset featuring annotations of variable descriptions and values extracted from a corpus of scientific literature about COVID-19 and earth sciences. Utilizing this annotated dataset, we have comprehensively evaluated the most popular LLMs, machine learning models, and their combinations, assessing their effectiveness in identifying and extracting this critical information.

3 Variable Extractions Dataset

The benchmark comprises excerpts extracted from 22 papers that focus on pandemic research, specifically available at the benchmark repository[3] These papers typically introduce at least one epidemiological model, providing detailed descriptions and evaluations of the models and their variables. Collectively, the research papers address the challenge of modeling and forecasting the spread of COVID-19 under various scenarios and interventions. They explore a range of modeling approaches, including standard models like SIR and SEIR, as well as more complex frameworks such as COVID-ABS and Covasim. These models are used to analyze the effects of government interventions and to predict the trajectory of the pandemic in different regions. In addition, studies emphasize the extraction and annotation of relevant variables and parameters from the literature, with the aim of enhancing the precision and applicability of these epidemiological models in real-world scenarios.

3.1 Human Annotation

In our study, we meticulously annotated a set of documents to facilitate the extraction and analysis of scientific variables and their contextual data. The annotation process was designed to capture three primary types of information: (1) variable names and their descriptions, (2) variable names paired with their corresponding values, and (3) additional metadata, including model card attributes and scenario card attributes. Detailed guidelines for these annotation task are described in Appendix A.

3.1.1 Annotation Process

Annotation requires expertise in mathematical modeling of epidemics, making our current annotations challenging to obtain. Human annotators were tasked with identifying and labeling specific elements in the text according to the following categories:

[3]https://github.com/mitdbg/scivar

Variables with Values: Annotators highlighted instances where a variable was directly associated with a numerical value or a range of values. This includes cases where the variable might be implied rather than explicitly stated. For example, annotators would mark the phrase "the estimated reproduction rate in the United States was around 2.5" to capture the variable (reproduction rate) and its value (2.5).

Variable Descriptions: This task involved identifying and highlighting descriptions of variables that explain or define the variable within the context of the document. For instance, the phrase "lambda represents the infection coefficient" would be annotated to link the variable lambda with its description.

3.1.2 Annotation Standards and Tools

The annotation was performed using Adobe Acrobat, which allowed annotators to use different colors to distinguish between the types of annotations, as specified in the guidelines. The standards for annotation emphasized precision, instructing annotators to prioritize accuracy in identifying and marking text elements. Generous alignment standards were applied during the evaluation of the annotations, focusing on the relevance and completeness of the information captured rather than strict adherence to text boundaries.

3.1.3 Quality Control

To ensure the quality and consistency of the annotations, each document underwent a review process. Annotations that were missed or incorrectly marked in the initial round were identified and corrected. This iterative process helped refine the annotations and improve the overall accuracy of the data set.

3.1.4 Post-Processing with Structured Format

After the annotation and quality review process, each paper will have a unified color code mapping for different annotation categories. We utilize pdfannots[4] tool to extract the PDF annotations into JSON format, categorizing the entries and their text spans from the original text. Pdfannots is a program that extracts annotations (highlights, comments, etc.).

For each annotation, we obtain the highlighted text and its surrounding context into a text passage. We aggregated passages shared by multiple annotations to remove redundancy, for example, a

[4]https://github.com/0xabu/pdfannots

```
{
  "all_text": "1 + αR can be thought of as S + I + R + αR. Given
  ↪ that S + I + R = 1, this is equivalent to the usual form 1 +
  ↪ αR. Figure 1 illustrates shield immunity impacts on a SIR
  ↪ epidemic with (R0 = 2.5) (R0 is the basic reproduction
  ↪ number). In this SIR model, shield immunity reduces the
  ↪ epidemic peak and shortens the duration of epidemic spread.
  ↪ Shielding in this context acts as a negative feedback loop,
  ↪ given that the effective reproduction number is given by
  ↪ Reff(t) / R0 = S(t) / (1 + αR(t)). As a result, interaction
  ↪ substitution increases as recovered individuals increase in
  ↪ number and are identified. For example, in the case of (α =
  ↪ 20), the epidemic concludes with less than 20% infected in
  ↪ contrast to the final size of ~90% in the baseline scenario
  ↪ without shielding (Fig. 2).",
  "page": 2,
  "annotations": [
    [185, 193, "R0 = 2.5", "var val"],
    [195, 232, "(R0 is the basic reproduction number)", "var desc"],
    [634, 640, "α = 20", "var val"]
  ],
  "file": "epidemic_model_analysis"
}
```

Figure 2: Example of SciVar JSON output extracted and formatted from an annotated PDF text block in Figure 1.

paragraph containing several variable descriptions will appear only once in the dataset with all its associated annotations attached. From the 22 scientific papers, we have collected 556 text chunks containing 2083 variable-related annotations (1236 for variable descriptions and 847 for variable values). Each text block is configured with a set of annotations, which include character index and span, text extraction, and annotation type. An example of the structured JSON output can be seen in Figure 2.

This post-processing step ensures that the annotations are not only accurately and automated captured but also structured in a way that facilitates further analysis and application in information extraction systems and other research tools.

4 Variable Extraction Approaches

In our evaluation, we utilized diverse approaches, including traditional rule-based extraction models, popular LLMs with varying degrees of enhancement, and an optimized AI pipeline framework.

4.1 Rule-based Information Extraction

We developed a rule-based information extraction system[5] using the Odin language (Valenzuela-Escárcega et al., 2016) to identify and extract variables mentioned in text alongside their associated definitions or descriptions and values associated with them. The rule-based system operates by matching patterns over the syntax of a sentence or phrase. Figure 3 depicts an example rule. With the help of a linguist, we designed a set of rules to match different ways in which a concept or symbol (the variable) is defined (the description) in scientific papers. Similarly, another subset of rules to match numerical values and quantities associated to variables. Rule-based information extraction tools serve as complement to LLM and other deep-learning based approaches. They trade generalization and recall capabilities for higher precision and interpretability.

```
1 - name: description_interpreted
2   label: Description
3   priority: ${priority}
4   type: dependency
5   example: "Beta can be interpreted
      ↪ as the effective contact rate."
6   pattern: |
7       trigger = [lemma="interpret"]
8       description:Phrase = nmod_as
9       variable:Identifier = nsubjpass
```

Figure 3: Example of a pattern-matching rule system designed to detect variable descriptions. The word `interpreted` will anchor the pattern (line 8). Outgoing syntactic dependencies of types `nmod_as` and `nsubjpass` to entities of types `Phrase` and `Identifier` link the rule's trigger to its description and variable arguments, respectively.

4.2 Vanilla LLM Extraction

LLMs have demonstrated exceptional performance on a variety of semantic information extraction tasks. In our study, we established LLM baselines using a vanilla pipeline, in which each LLM was provided with only snippets of text on paper and tasked with extracting variable names, descriptions, and values. To optimize the effectiveness of our approach, we conducted extensive prompt engineering, iterating through more than ten rounds of refinement. These prompts were developed by a team of four PhD or postdoctoral researchers in computer science major, and the most effective prompt was selected for use in our evaluations. Figure 4 illustrates the prompt template that was used in all LLM baselines. In this template, `[]` serves as a placeholder for the paper text, and the prompt specifies a structured format for the output, with default values provided for optional fields. Additionally, we incorporate a few-shot prompting setup that provides language models with several examples within the prompt to enhance their performance.

[5] `https://github.com/ml4ai/skema/tree/main/skema/text_reading/scala`

4.3 Tool Enhanced LLM Extraction

LLMs often share similar technical frameworks and have substantial overlap in their training datasets. This commonality can lead them to either overemphasize or overlook certain cases. To mitigate these biases and enhance extraction accuracy, it is beneficial to introduce additional perspectives. Therefore, beyond the standard evaluation using only the paper text, we have also incorporated outputs from a traditional model into our LLM evaluations. This approach is conceptually similar to the tool integration methods used in LangChain (Topsakal and Akinci, 2023); however, our objective is to generate a broader range of candidate options rather than to rely on the presumed high-quality outputs of these tools. As illustrated in Figure 4, these outputs are highlighted in blue font. The `[TOOL EXTRACTION]` provided by the traditional model offers supplementary variable options for consideration. However, in cases of discrepancy, the original text is always prioritized to ensure the fidelity of the information extracted.

Prompt: Please extract variable names and descriptions from the following paper text. You may refer to the provided tool extractions for your reference. Here is some paper text:
[TEXT]
This text may contain model related variables or parameters, their initial values and what they mean. If it does, list each of the variables on a separate line with the following attributes separated by "|":
name | description | numerical value.
If the variable's value uses other variables or there is no value for the variable, output "None" for that variable value; do not hallucinate a variable value or variable description that does not exist in the text.
[OPTIONAL_EXAMPLES]
Meanwhile, we get some variable extractions from another tool for your reference. These extractions may contain false positive or duplication cases. Please pay more attention to the true positive variables:
[TOOL_EXTRACTION]
Please try to extract variables on the original paper text first, then refer to the results from the tool extractions and see if you miss any variables. If you are not sure, please always check the original paper text.

Figure 4: Prompt templates for variable extraction using various setups. The black font indicates the prompt template for a standard LLM. The combination of black and brown fonts represents the template for few-shot prompting. The integration of black and blue fonts denotes the template enhanced by external tools.

```
import palimpzest as pz

class Variable(pz.Schema):
    """ Represents a variable of a model in a scientific paper"""
    excerptid = pz.Field(desc="The unique identifier for the excerpt",
    ↪ required=True)
    name = pz.Field(desc="The label used for the scientific variable,
    ↪ like alpha or beta", required=True)
    description = pz.Field(desc="A description of the variable",
    ↪ required=False)
    value = pz.Field(desc="The value of the variable", required=False)

# define logical plan
excerpts = pz.Dataset("snippets", schema=pz.TextFile)
output = excerpts.convert(Variable, desc="A variable used or
↪ introduced in the paper snippet", cardinality="oneToMany")

# user specified policy and execute plan
policy = pz.MinimizeCostAtFixedQuality(min_quality=0.45)
results = pz.Execute(excerpts, policy=policy)
```

Figure 5: Palimpzest Code for Variable Extraction from Scientific Paper Snippets.

4.4 Optimized AI Pipeline Framework

We also incorporate a system featuring a simple and declarative user interface. Palimpzest is a system designed to streamline AI-powered analytics through declarative query processing (Liu et al., 2024). This system allows users to effortlessly specify analytical queries over unstructured data using a straightforward, Python-embedded declarative language. Users can define their desired data schema and attributes in natural language, enabling Palimpzest to automate complex optimization processes. This automation includes navigating various AI models, employing prompting techniques, and optimizing foundational models, thereby eliminating the need for the laborious tasks of manual pipeline tuning, model selection, and prompt engineering previously required when working with LLMs. By efficiently managing trade-offs between runtime, cost, and data quality, Palimpzest simplifies user interaction and significantly enhances the efficiency and cost-effectiveness of processing large-scale data. These capabilities position Palimpzest as a robust benchmark for evaluating the performance of AI-driven data processing systems in scientific and analytical contexts, ensuring substantial improvements in execution times and costs while maintaining or enhancing data quality.

The Palimpzest code snippet shown in Figure 5 demonstrates a declarative approach to extracting variables from scientific paper excerpts. It defines the 'Variable' class, which details a scientific variable found within the paper excerpt. This class includes fields for the variable's name, description, and value, with only the variable name being required. This setup efficiently captures the essential details needed for variable extraction, streamlining the process of transforming unstructured text into structured data suitable for further analysis.

The code then creates a dataset named "snippets" with the Palimpzest native 'TextFile' schema and processes it to convert each snippet into instances of the 'Variable' class, identifying variables mentioned in the text. This conversion cardinality 'oneToMany' allows for multiple variables per snippet, reflecting the typical structure of scientific excerpts.

Finally, a user-specified policy ('MinimizeCostAtFixedQuality') is set to optimize the extraction process by minimizing operational costs while maintaining the quality of the extracted data above a predetermined threshold. The 'Execute' function applies this policy to the dataset, demonstrating how Palimpzest simplifies complex data extraction tasks through its declarative programming model.

5 Evaluation

5.1 Experimental Setup

We evaluate a variety of models to assess their performance on the variable extraction dataset. The traditional rule-based model is denoted as `rules`, and an optimized AI pipeline framework is referred to as `Palimpzest`. Additionally, we examine several advanced models from OpenAI, including `GPT3.5 Turbo`, `GPT4 Turbo`, `GPT4o`, and `GPT4o-mini`. We also test two locally served LLMs, `Llama-3-8B-Instruct` and `Mistral-7B-Instruct-v0.2`, which are integrated via vLLM model serving APIs. Each LLM is evaluated using a standard API call, indicated by the prefix *pure_*, and an enhanced version that incorporates outputs from the traditional model, indicated by the prefix *tool_*. The LLM temperature parameter is set to zero to ensure reproducibility.

We executed all baseline models using the prompts or configurations outlined in the previous section. The results are then aligned with the human-annotated ground truth, as illustrated in Figure 2. This alignment is based on the input text chunk ID. Furthermore, we construct all possible candidate pairs by applying the Cartesian product to the sets of predicted extractions and ground truth, grouped by annotation type. This process resulted in a total of $330,558$ candidate pairs for evaluation. For each candidate pair, we employed a set of evaluation metrics to determine whether it qualified as a match.

To evaluate the F1 score in our study, we meticulously track the ground truth and prediction sets for each text chunk. During the evaluation process, when an evaluator confirms a match (though the criteria for a match may vary across different metrics), the index of the matched candidate pair is recorded in both the ground truth and prediction entries for that specific pair. After evaluating all candidate pairs associated with a given text chunk, we calculate the recall as the ratio of entries with at least one match in the ground truth set. Similarly, precision is calculated as the ratio of entries with at least one match in the prediction set. The F1 score is then computed using the harmonic mean of precision and recall, providing a balanced measure of the model's accuracy in variable extraction tasks. In cases where the evaluation focuses on specific tasks, such as variable descriptions or variable values extraction only, we count only the corresponding entries and disregard the others.

5.2 GPT-4 as a Similarity Evaluator

We employed the GPT-4 turbo model to perform similarity evaluations, comparing its outputs with a ground-truth dataset to assess precision and accuracy across different tasks. Depending on whether the candidate pair being evaluated corresponds to "var_desc" or "var_val" (examples provided in Figure 2), we use specific prompts as illustrated in Figure 6. To ensure conciseness, we limit the output token length to one.

Prompt for Variable Description/Value:

You are a human evaluator. The following pair of text describes a variable and its description/value.
[VAR_DESC_A]/[VAR_VAL_A]
[VAR_DESC_B]/[VAR_VAL_B]
Please check if they mean the same. Answer y or n.

Figure 6: GPT4 Turbo prompt templates for evaluating the consistency of variable descriptions and values.

According to Table 1, no existing solution performs exceptionally well on the variable extraction task. However, the integration of rule-based approaches with LLMs has shown significant improvements. The best-performing baseline model achieved an F1 score of only 0.491, while the integration with LLMs, particularly the GPT-4 variants, enhanced performance, achieving F1 scores as high as 0.525. This represents a 20% improvement over the setups using only LLMs, except for `GPT3.5T` where the integration did not yield a performance boost. Such integration highlights the complemen-

Table 1: Average performance with GPT4 similarity evolution with ground-truth (bold font indicates the best over each setup).

Model	Overall Performance			Variable Descriptions			Variable Values		
	Recall	Precision	F1	Recall	Precision	F1	Recall	Precision	F1
pure_GPT3.5T	0.576	0.337	0.393	0.677	0.361	0.431	0.404	0.305	0.323
tool_GPT3.5T	0.568	0.307	0.369 ↓	0.647	0.318	0.396	0.429	0.281	0.306
3shot_GPT3.5T	0.543	0.412	0.437 ↑	0.558	0.433	0.457	0.521	0.378	0.400
pure_GPT4T	0.655	0.443	**0.491**	0.708	0.428	0.495	0.527	0.460	0.456
tool_GPT4T	0.662	0.451	0.500 ↑	0.711	0.440	0.506	0.559	0.478	0.476
3shot_GPT4T	0.645	0.502	**0.535** ↑	0.650	0.471	0.514	0.629	0.557	0.553
pure_GPT4o	0.647	0.424	0.480	0.708	0.438	0.504	0.513	0.382	0.408
tool_GPT4o	0.689	0.460	0.520 ↑	0.727	0.453	0.526	0.589	0.468	0.483
3shot_GPT4o	0.499	0.360	0.389 ↓	0.486	0.376	0.395	0.525	0.369	0.397
pure_GPT4o-mini	0.619	0.376	0.437	0.693	0.410	0.479	0.499	0.325	0.360
tool_GPT4o-mini	0.694	0.465	**0.525** ↑	0.729	0.446	0.520	0.619	0.481	0.504
3shot_GPT4o-mini	0.545	0.322	0.378 ↓	0.578	0.370	0.426	0.475	0.231	0.282
pure_llama	0.600	0.402	0.446	0.671	0.422	0.483	0.456	0.373	0.372
tool_llama	0.629	0.396	0.451 ↑	0.706	0.411	0.482	0.479	0.354	0.369
3shot_llama	0.488	0.181	0.244 ↓	0.550	0.204	0.279	0.402	0.139	0.180
pure_mistral	0.572	0.234	0.301	0.661	0.220	0.302	0.404	0.285	0.310
tool_mistral	0.564	0.277	0.335 ↑	0.650	0.265	0.343	0.412	0.307	0.317
3shot_mistral	0.493	0.190	0.248 ↓	0.588	0.191	0.262	0.352	0.194	0.217
rules	0.392	0.317	0.320	0.447	0.352	0.358	0.299	0.244	0.245
Palimpzest	0.574	0.451	0.473	0.566	0.435	0.460	0.555	0.453	0.465
structured_GPT4o	0.64	0.443	0.492	0.682	0.435	0.498	0.535	0.446	0.449
structured_GPT4o-mini	0.658	0.424	0.484	0.689	0.406	0.476	0.593	0.442	0.473

tary strengths of diverse methodologies: rule-based approaches provide additional variable extraction options from different perspectives, thereby enhancing the performance of LLMs.

Among the models tested, the tool-enhanced versions generally outperformed their pure counterparts, with tool_GPT4o-mini achieving the highest F1 score of 0.525. This indicates that the additional suggestions provided by tool extractions can effectively guide LLMs to achieve better performance. In contrast, the rule-based approach alone (rules) demonstrated lower effectiveness, with an F1 score of 0.320, emphasizing the overall superior capability of LLM-based solutions in managing complex extraction tasks.

However, few-shot prompting does not consistently yield improved extraction results, as indicated by Table 1. Only GPT3.5T and GPT4T models showed improvement with the few-shot setting, while others experienced diminished performance. This variability could be attributed to the inherent complexity of the variable extraction task, where the diverse scenarios may not benefit significantly from a few additional examples. Moreover, the inclusion of more tokens in the prompt might dilute the attention mechanism, thereby worsening the results.

The Palimpzest system, utilizing GPT-4o as its conversion model, yielded results comparable to pure_GPT4o, achieving an F1 score of 0.473. By enforcing a strict format constraint, Palimpzest trades some recall for higher precision, offering a more reliable output without the need for extensive model selection and prompt engineering. This approach not only simplifies the extraction process but also enhances the usability and applicability of the system in practical scenarios, establishing a robust foundation for automatic model recovery and simulation.

Additionally, we conducted a distinct quality assessment for both variable descriptions and variable values, with detailed results presented in Table 1. The observations mentioned above remain consistent across these evaluations. However, almost all baselines demonstrated better F1 scores on the variable descriptions task compared to their overall performance, with the exception of Palimpzest, which excelled in both cases in general but performed slightly better in the variable value extraction task.

5.3 Token-based Evaluation

In addition to the GPT-based evaluation, we examined the token-level precision, recall and F1 scores used for QA and other span prediction NLP tasks (Rajpurkar et al., 2016). Token-level scores account for the correct number of tokens predicted by each method, giving credit based on the proportion of tokens predicted correctly and penalizing for tokens predicted incorrectly. Table 2 shows the token level performance on the variable extrac-

Table 2: Average token-level scores for variable descriptions and variable values.

Model	Overall Performance			Variable Descriptions			Variable Values		
	Recall	**Precision**	**F1**	**Recall**	**Precision**	**F1**	**Recall**	**Precision**	**F1**
pure_GPT3.5T	0.622	0.578	0.552	0.730	0.663	0.645	0.458	0.449	0.410
tool_GPT3.5T	0.551	0.527	0.505 ↓	0.636	0.625	0.599	0.421	0.379	0.362
3shot_GPT3.5T	0.514	0.492	0.467 ↓	0.560	0.486	0.483	0.444	0.499	0.443
pure_GPT4T	0.661	0.587	0.571	0.770	0.670	0.666	0.496	0.460	0.428
tool_GPT4T	0.667	0.638	0.610 ↑	0.771	0.712	0.695	0.508	0.527	0.482
3shot_GPT4T	0.638	0.585	0.562 ↓	0.733	0.623	0.623	0.493	0.527	0.471
pure_GPT4o	0.664	0.621	0.595	0.759	0.688	0.673	0.521	0.520	0.477
tool_GPT4o	0.667	0.620	0.599 ↑	0.768	0.686	0.681	0.513	0.521	0.475
3shot_GPT4o	0.541	0.512	0.487 ↓	0.557	0.488	0.482	0.517	0.548	0.495
pure_GPT4o-mini	0.645	0.641	**0.600**	0.766	0.701	0.686	0.463	0.549	0.470
tool_GPT4o-mini	0.659	0.691	**0.640** ↑	0.771	0.773	0.738	0.489	0.567	0.490
3shot_GPT4o-mini	0.644	0.589	**0.564** ↓	0.703	0.579	0.586	0.556	0.604	0.532
pure_llama	0.614	0.599	0.557	0.712	0.718	0.672	0.465	0.417	0.383
tool_llama	0.621	0.630	0.585 ↑	0.723	0.780	0.716	0.466	0.401	0.385
3shot_llama	0.554	0.553	0.511 ↓	0.614	0.607	0.573	0.461	0.470	0.417
pure_mistral	0.609	0.486	0.488	0.718	0.583	0.591	0.444	0.340	0.332
tool_mistral	0.508	0.450	0.435 ↓	0.606	0.551	0.532	0.359	0.295	0.288
3shot_mistral	0.564	0.489	0.482 ↓	0.693	0.592	0.592	0.369	0.332	0.316
rules	0.429	0.498	0.437	0.494	0.583	0.505	0.329	0.369	0.335
Palimpzest	0.569	0.513	0.488	0.648	0.527	0.526	0.448	0.490	0.431

tion dataset. The results don't diverge significantly from the GPT-based evaluation and consistently highlight the strength of LLM-based methods. Crucially, token-level scores rely solely on manual annotations, therefore any conclusions drawn from them are based only on the ground truth and not subject to any potential inaccuracies from a model-based evaluation.

5.4 Full Paper Context Extraction Evaluation

We conducted variable extraction evaluations using the full text of each of the 22 articles. This approach limits the number of language models that can be used due to the token limits imposed by many LLMs. We present the results of a rule-based model, GPT-3.5T (with chunking the long text into chunks within the model limit) , and GPT-4T. The overall performance is shown in Table 3.

When dealing with the extensive context of a scientific paper, LLMs can struggle to maintain focus, often resulting in lower recall. In contrast, the rules and pure_GPT3.5T_C with chunking options manage to maintain relatively high recall. Overall, even in the context of lengthy texts, integrating tool outputs helps LLMs concentrate on the extraction task, leading to improved results.

Table 3: Overall Performance with Full Paper Text on Selected Models

Model	Recall	Precision	F1
rules	0.701	0.101	0.172
pure_GPT3.5T_C	0.750	0.250	0.340
pure_GPT4T	0.564	0.488	0.490
tool_GPT4T	0.678	0.467	**0.506**

6 Conclusion

We have introduced a dataset for extracting variable descriptions and values from scientific literature, a crucial building block for the automated recovery of mathematical models from the literature. We conducted a battery of evaluations using different commercial and open-source LLMs, a rule-based information extraction system, and a declarative AI pipeline framework. In our experiments, we found that LLM-based methods tend to be the most effective methods to identify and extract variable descriptions and values; however, testing ensembles of rule-based and LLM-based information extractions working in tandem, boost the performance yield the best results most of the time. Considering that all the methods tested in this work did not use any form of supervised learning, there is ample room for improvement. In future work, multiple interesting avenues for research can be explored: Using semi-supervised and data-augmentation methods to augment the size of the dataset, and the use of supervised fine-tuning of encoder-based language models for generation and token prediction can improve the accuracy of the results.

7 Acknowledgments

We would like to express our gratitude for the support provided by the DARPA ASKEM Award HR00112220042. Additionally, we extend our appreciation to Patty Gahan and Robyn Kozierok from MITRE for their diligent annotation efforts.

8 Limitations

We recognize that our work has certain limitations. As is common in research involving human annotations, budget and labor constraints have resulted in a relatively small dataset compared to those constructed using automatic or semi-automatic methods. Moreover, the occurrence of mathematical variable descriptions and values within natural language text is inherently sparse due to the nature of the articles we analyzed. Additionally, our study focuses exclusively on English literature, which may limit its generalizability to other languages.

Despite the small size of our dataset, it was curated by multiple domain experts following a well-defined annotation protocol, ensuring high quality. We hope that by releasing this dataset, we can inspire future efforts to curate larger datasets and foster new research in this area.

9 Ethical Considerations

All of the articles annotated in our dataset are published with an open access license. We identify the papers in Appendix B.

References

Qian Chen, Zhu Zhuo, and Wen Wang. 2019. Bert for joint intent classification and slot filling. *ArXiv*, abs/1902.10909.

Zui Chen, Lei Cao, Sam Madden, Tim Kraska, Zeyuan Shang, Ju Fan, Nan Tang, Zihui Gu, Chunwei Liu, and Michael Cafarella. 2023. Seed: Domain-specific data curation with large language models. *arXiv e-prints*, pages arXiv–2310.

Jacob Collard, Valeria de Paiva, Brendan Fong, and Eswaran Subrahmanian. 2022. Extracting mathematical concepts from text. In *Proceedings of the Eighth Workshop on Noisy User-generated Text (W-NUT 2022)*, pages 15–23, Gyeongju, Republic of Korea. Association for Computational Linguistics.

Sabina Jeschke, Marc Wilke, Marie Blanke, Nicole M. Natho, and Olivier F. Pfeiffer. 2007. Information extraction from mathematical texts by means of natural language processing techniques. In *Proceedings of the International Workshop on Educational Multimedia and Multimedia Education*, Emme '07, page 109–114, New York, NY, USA. Association for Computing Machinery.

Albert Q. Jiang, Alexandre Sablayrolles, Arthur Mensch, Chris Bamford, Devendra Singh Chaplot, Diego de las Casas, Florian Bressand, Gianna Lengyel, Guillaume Lample, Lucile Saulnier, Lélio Renard Lavaud, Marie-Anne Lachaux, Pierre Stock, Teven Le Scao, Thibaut Lavril, Thomas Wang, Timothée Lacroix, and William El Sayed. 2023. Mistral 7b. *Preprint*, arXiv:2310.06825.

Jin-Dong Kim, Yue Wang, and Yamamoto Yasunori. 2013. The Genia event extraction shared task, 2013 edition - overview. In *Proceedings of the BioNLP Shared Task 2013 Workshop*, pages 8–15, Sofia, Bulgaria. Association for Computational Linguistics.

Ni Lao, Tom Mitchell, and William W. Cohen. 2011. Random walk inference and learning in a large scale knowledge base. In *Proceedings of the 2011 Conference on Empirical Methods in Natural Language Processing*, pages 529–539, Edinburgh, Scotland, UK. Association for Computational Linguistics.

Yiming Lin, Madelon Hulsebos, Ruiying Ma, Shreya Shankar, Sepanta Zeigham, Aditya G Parameswaran, and Eugene Wu. 2024. Towards accurate and efficient document analytics with large language models. *arXiv preprint arXiv:2405.04674*.

Chunwei Liu, Matthew Russo, Michael Cafarella, Lei Cao, Peter Baile Chen, Zui Chen, Michael Franklin, Tim Kraska, Samuel Madden, Rana Shahout, et al. 2025. Palimpzest: Optimizing ai-powered analytics with declarative query processing. In *CIDR 2025*.

Chunwei Liu, Matthew Russo, Michael Cafarella, Lei Cao, Peter Baille Chen, Zui Chen, Michael Franklin, Tim Kraska, Samuel Madden, and Gerardo Vitagliano. 2024. A declarative system for optimizing ai workloads. *Preprint*, arXiv:2405.14696.

Sunil Mohan and Donghui Li. 2019. Medmentions: A large biomedical corpus annotated with UMLS concepts. *CoRR*, abs/1902.09476.

Mark Neumann, Daniel King, Iz Beltagy, and Waleed Ammar. 2019. ScispaCy: Fast and Robust Models for Biomedical Natural Language Processing. In *Proceedings of the 18th BioNLP Workshop and Shared Task*, pages 319–327, Florence, Italy. Association for Computational Linguistics.

Enrique Noriega-Atala, Md. Rahat-Uz-Zaman, Ruchika Bhat, Mladen Jergovic, Stephen G. Kobourov, and Janko Nikolich-Zugich. 2023. Visualizing interaction networks and evidence in biomedical corpora. In *2023 IEEE 16th Pacific Visualization Symposium (PacificVis)*, pages 41–50.

Tomoko Ohta, Sampo Pyysalo, Rafal Rak, Andrew Rowley, Hong-Woo Chun, Sung-Jae Jung, Sung-Pil Choi, Sophia Ananiadou, and Jun'ichi Tsujii.

2013. Overview of the pathway curation (PC) task of BioNLP shared task 2013. In *Proceedings of the BioNLP Shared Task 2013 Workshop*, pages 67–75, Sofia, Bulgaria. Association for Computational Linguistics.

OpenAI. 2024. Gpt-4 technical report. *Preprint*, arXiv:2303.08774.

Liana Patel, Siddharth Jha, Carlos Guestrin, and Matei Zaharia. 2024. Lotus: Enabling semantic queries with llms over tables of unstructured and structured data. *arXiv preprint arXiv:2407.11418*.

Adarsh Pyarelal, Marco Antonio Valenzuela-Escárcega, Rebecca Sharp, Paul Douglas Hein, Jon Stephens, Pratik Bhandari, HeuiChan Lim, Saumya Debray, and Clayton T. Morrison. 2020. Automates: Automated model assembly from text, equations, and software. *CoRR*, abs/2001.07295.

Pranav Rajpurkar, Jian Zhang, Konstantin Lopyrev, and Percy Liang. 2016. SQuAD: 100,000+ questions for machine comprehension of text. In *Proceedings of the 2016 Conference on Empirical Methods in Natural Language Processing*, pages 2383–2392, Austin, Texas. Association for Computational Linguistics.

Tarek Saier, Mayumi Ohta, Takuto Asakura, and Michael Färber. 2024. Hyperpie: Hyperparameter information extraction from scientific publications. In *European Conference on Information Retrieval*, pages 254–269. Springer.

Timo Schaffhauser, Daniel Garijo, Maximiliano Osorio, Daniel Bittner, Suzanne Pierce, Hernán Vargas, Markus Disse, and Yolanda Gil. 2023. A framework for the broad dissemination of hydrological models for non-expert users. *Environmental Modelling & Software*, 164:105695.

Rebecca Sharp, Adarsh Pyarelal, Benjamin Gyori, Keith Alcock, Egoitz Laparra, Marco A. Valenzuela-Escárcega, Ajay Nagesh, Vikas Yadav, John Bachman, Zheng Tang, Heather Lent, Fan Luo, Mithun Paul, Steven Bethard, Kobus Barnard, Clayton Morrison, and Mihai Surdeanu. 2019. Eidos, INDRA, & delphi: From free text to executable causal models. In *Proceedings of the 2019 Conference of the North American Chapter of the Association for Computational Linguistics (Demonstrations)*, pages 42–47, Minneapolis, Minnesota. Association for Computational Linguistics.

Anastasia Shimorina, Johannes Heinecke, and Frédéric Herledan. 2022. Knowledge extraction from texts based on Wikidata. In *Proceedings of the 2022 Conference of the North American Chapter of the Association for Computational Linguistics: Human Language Technologies: Industry Track*, pages 297–304, Hybrid: Seattle, Washington + Online. Association for Computational Linguistics.

Erik F. Tjong Kim Sang and Fien De Meulder. 2003. Introduction to the CoNLL-2003 shared task: Language-independent named entity recognition. In *Proceedings of the Seventh Conference on Natural Language Learning at HLT-NAACL 2003*, pages 142–147.

Oguzhan Topsakal and Tahir Cetin Akinci. 2023. Creating large language model applications utilizing langchain: A primer on developing llm apps fast. In *International Conference on Applied Engineering and Natural Sciences*, volume 1, pages 1050–1056.

Hugo Touvron, Thibaut Lavril, Gautier Izacard, Xavier Martinet, Marie-Anne Lachaux, Timothée Lacroix, Baptiste Rozière, Naman Goyal, Eric Hambro, Faisal Azhar, Aurelien Rodriguez, Armand Joulin, Edouard Grave, and Guillaume Lample. 2023. Llama: Open and efficient foundation language models. *Preprint*, arXiv:2302.13971.

Marco A Valenzuela-Escárcega, Özgün Babur, Gus Hahn-Powell, Dane Bell, Thomas Hicks, Enrique Noriega-Atala, Xia Wang, Mihai Surdeanu, Emek Demir, and Clayton T Morrison. 2018. Large-scale automated machine reading discovers new cancer-driving mechanisms. *Database*, 2018:bay098.

Marco A. Valenzuela-Escárcega, Gus Hahn-Powell, and Mihai Surdeanu. 2016. Odin's runes: A rule language for information extraction. In *Proceedings of the Tenth International Conference on Language Resources and Evaluation (LREC'16)*, pages 322–329, Portorož, Slovenia. European Language Resources Association (ELRA).

Yanshan Wang, Liwei Wang, Majid Rastegar-Mojarad, Sungrim Moon, Feichen Shen, Naveed Afzal, Sijia Liu, Yuqun Zeng, Saeed Mehrabi, Sunghwan Sohn, and Hongfang Liu. 2018. Clinical information extraction applications: A literature review. *Journal of Biomedical Informatics*, 77:34–49.

Derong Xu, Wei Chen, Wenjun Peng, Chao Zhang, Tong Xu, Xiangyu Zhao, Xian Wu, Yefeng Zheng, Yang Wang, and Enhong Chen. 2024. Large language models for generative information extraction: A survey. *Preprint*, arXiv:2312.17617.

Kristianto Giovanni Yoko, Minh-Quoc Nghiem, Yuichiroh Matsubayashi, and Akiko AIZAWA. 2012. Extracting definitions of mathematical expressions in scientific papers. *The 26th Annual Conference of the Japanese Society for Artificial Intelligence*, JSAI2012:3P1IOS2a3–3P1IOS2a3.

Yuhao Zhang, Victor Zhong, Danqi Chen, Gabor Angeli, and Christopher D. Manning. 2017. Position-aware attention and supervised data improve slot filling. In *Proceedings of the 2017 Conference on Empirical Methods in Natural Language Processing (EMNLP 2017)*, pages 35–45.

Lianmin Zheng, Liangsheng Yin, Zhiqiang Xie, Jeff Huang, Chuyue Sun, Cody Hao Yu, Shiyi Cao, Christos Kozyrakis, Ion Stoica, Joseph E Gonzalez, et al. 2023. Efficiently programming large language models using sglang. *arXiv preprint arXiv:2312.07104*.

A Annotation Guidelines

A.1 General Conventions

Annotators should prioritize precision over recall in their first round of annotation on each document. Annotations that are missed (i.e., elements that should be annotated but haven't been) can be corrected upon document review. The task is to identify all instances of such expressions in each text, including in the title, abstract, and figure and table captions. Figures, tables, keywords, floating equations, acknowledgment sections, and references, however, are not annotated.

A.2 Nested Annotations

"Nested annotations" can happen when annotators tag nested elements that occur within the boundaries of a longer annotation. This task prioritizes tagging the longest extent of an expression in cases of overlapping annotation. For example, in the "variable with value" expression below, "United States" is not tagged even though it is a "location context."

- `the [estimated reproduction rate in the United States as a whole stood at around 2.5].`

A.3 Events

The evaluation will use generous alignment standards that do not require exactly matching extents but it is preferable, though not mandatory, to exclude white space and punctuation when annotating.

A.4 Annotation Types

Annotators are asked to use assigned colors to highlight five different types of annotations: Variables with Values, Variable Descriptions, Locations and Temporal Contexts, and Model Card annotations. The guidelines below provide further instructions for each annotation type.

Variables with Values

This entity type captures variables with their numeric values. Values expressed as ranges should be annotated. To qualify as a Variable with Value, the expression must contain a number assigned to a simple expression.

This entity type is marked in blue. Some examples include:

- growth rate of 0.01
- r0 = 1.2
- Reproduction numbers of COVID-19 vary in different studies and regions of the world (in addition over time) but have generally been found to be between 1.5 and 6.
- the estimated reproduction rate in the United States as a whole stood at around 2.5.
- The number of unquarantined infected cases was 1200.
- Beta represents a value 1-3

Do annotate a value expression as a Variable with Value even when the variable is implied, and not explicit. Annotate and then add a pop-up note to indicate the implied variable. For example, "334" would be annotated as a Variable with Value and then noted as "Implied variable: unquarantined infected cases."

- The number of unquarantined infected cases was 1200. The number[6] had been 334.

Do not include confidence intervals in the extent of the variable with value expression:

- the mean control reproductive number is 6.47 (95% CI 5.71-7.3)

Do not tag equations as variables with values.

- $I(t) = Io_e^{xt}$

Variable Descriptions

This entity type captures descriptions of variables. In the case of complex phrases, highlight the whole span of text that contains the complete information. This entity type is highlighted in yellow. Some examples include:

- lambda represents the infection coefficient
- infected (asymptomatic or pauci-symptomatic infected, undetected)
- B is the number of such variables
- y is the recovery rate constant
- S is the total number of infected
- normalized infection i

[6]The number refers to the unquarantined infected cases. As such, this is a way to handle coreference with implied variables.

- I infections
- time $Td = ln2/\alpha$
- Hp is the Hubble constant
- Susceptible, Exposed, Infectious versus S Susceptible, E Exposed, I Infectious

Do not tag vacuous expressions as variable descriptions, such as:

- parameter v

B Dataset Articles

Table 4 contains the list of DOIs of the articles annotated to create the variable descriptions and values dataset.

DOI
10.1073/pnas.2112532119
10.1287/opre.2022.2306
10.1101/2020.04.09.20047498
10.1016/j.chaos.2020.110088
10.1371/journal.pcbi.1009149
10.1038/s41591-020-0883-7
10.1073/pnas.2006520117
10.1016/j.idm.2020.03.001
10.1016/j.chaos.2020.109846
10.1371/journal.pone.0236386
10.3390/ijerph18179027
10.1038/s41467-020-20544-y
10.1038/s41598-022-06159-x
10.1016/j.physa.2020.125498
10.1007/s40484-020-0199-0
10.1038/s41591-020-0895-3
10.1186/s13104-020-05192-1
10.1016/j.healthplace.2020.102404
10.3390/jcm9020462
10.1016/j.idm.2020.02.001
10.1175/JPO-D-20-0286.1
10.1002/jmv.25827

Table 4: Digital Object Identifiers (DOI) of the articles used to build the annotations of the dataset.

How Well Do Large Language Models Extract Keywords? A Systematic Evaluation on Scientific Corpora

Nacef Ben Mansour
Sorbonne Université
Paris, France

Hamed Rahimi
ISIR, Sorbonne Université
Paris, France

Motasem Alrahabi*
ObTIC, Sorbonne Université
Paris, France

Abstract

Automatic keyword extraction from scientific articles is pivotal for organizing scholarly archives, powering semantic search engines, and mapping interdisciplinary research trends. However, existing methods—including statistical and graph-based approaches—struggle to handle domain-specific challenges such as technical terminology, cross-disciplinary ambiguity, and dynamic scientific jargon. This paper presents an empirical comparison of traditional keyword extraction methods (e.g. TextRank and YAKE) with approaches based on Large Language Model. We introduce a novel evaluation framework that combines fuzzy semantic matching based on Levenshtein Distance with exact-match metrics (F1, precision, recall) to address inconsistencies in keyword normalization across scientific corpora. Through an extensive ablation study across nine different LLMs, we analyze their performance and associated costs. Our findings reveal that LLM-based methods consistently achieve superior precision and relevance compared to traditional approaches. This performance advantage suggests significant potential for improving scientific search systems and information retrieval in academic contexts.

1 Introduction

Keyword extraction algorithms are a group of statistical techniques that aim to identify the most relevant and representative terms for documents (Firoozeh et al., 2020). These methods have a wide range of applications, from improving information retrieval (Bracewell et al., 2005) and search engine optimization (Horasan, 2021) to information extraction, automatic document summarization (Bharti and Babu, 2017), and emerging trend detection (Kim et al., 2015). Over the years, the methodologies for keyword extraction have evolved significantly, reflecting advances in both linguistic understanding and computational techniques.

Traditional approaches, such as YAKE! (Campos et al., 2020), utilized syntactic analyses like noun or n-gram phrases to extract linguistic characteristics, including factors such as word position and frequency. Statistical techniques, including TF-IDF (Salton and Buckley, 1990) and RAKE (Rose et al., 2010), introduced quantitative measures to assess the importance of terms within a text and across corpora. While early methods primarily relied on linguistic rules and statistical measures, recent advancements have embraced deep learning to capture both contextual and semantic nuances. This shift has been driven by the emergence of large language models (LLMs) (Song et al., 2023a), which leverage the Transformer architecture (Vaswani, 2017) to understand and generate text with remarkable contextual depth. LLMs excel at modeling complex relationships within text, enabling precise keyword extraction through zero-shot, few-shot, or fine-tuned approaches. Unlike traditional extractive methods, which are confined to selecting explicit terms from the text, generative models can create or rephrase keywords that encapsulate the underlying meaning, even when such terms are absent in the original text. In (Song et al., 2023b), the authors evaluate the performance of ChatGPT and ChatGLM in extracting keyphrases without prior fine-tuning, highlighting their effectiveness in identifying relevant terms. Meanwhile, (Maragheh et al., 2023) explores a multi-stage approach to keyword extraction in an e-commerce setting, aiming to refine results by filtering out non-informative or sensitive keywords and mitigating hallucinations. In this work, we present a comprehensive analysis of keyword extraction methods by bridging traditional approaches and LLMs. Specifically, we conduct a comparative evaluation of these methodologies, examining their strengths, limitations, and practical applications. Our study employs two matching

*motasem.alrahabi@sorbonne-universite.fr

Proceedings of the 1st Workshop on AI and Scientific Discovery: Directions and Opportunities, pages 13–21
May 3, 2025

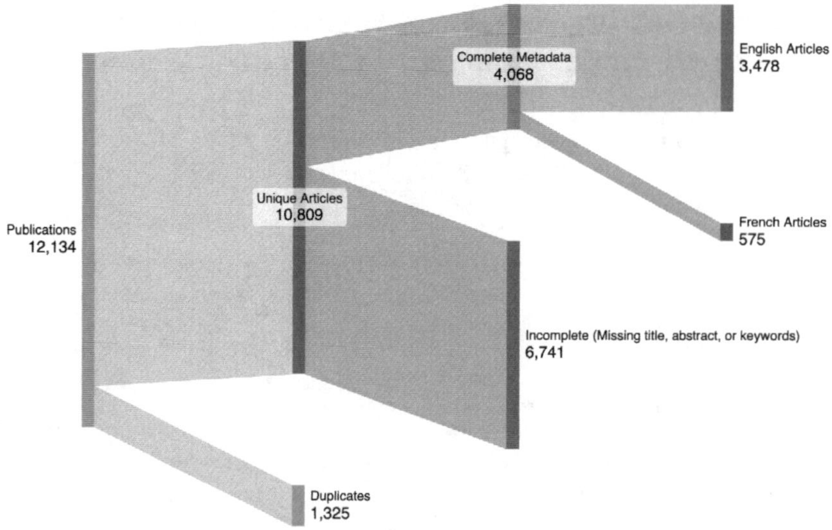

Figure 1: **Distribution of articles by language in HAL**

techniques—exact matching and flexible matching—to assess the effectiveness of keyword extraction. Furthermore, we perform an ablation study to investigate the performance and computational cost of different LLMs, providing insights into their trade-offs and suitability for various scenarios.

2 Related Works

The evolution of keyword extraction techniques has seen a diverse range of methods spanning supervised and unsupervised paradigms. Supervised approaches, such as classification-based algorithms, leverage annotated datasets to train models capable of identifying keywords. Notable examples include KP-Miner (El-Beltagy and Rafea, 2009) and the supervised framework by (Papagiannopoulou and Tsoumakas, 2020). In contrast, unsupervised methods, which do not rely on labeled data, have predominantly employed graph-based techniques. Algorithms such as TextRank (Mihalcea and Tarau, 2004), SingleRank (Wan and Xiao, 2008), and MultipartiteRank (Boudin, 2018) utilize word co-occurrence graphs to rank and extract keywords. Additionally, TopicRank (Bougouin et al., 2013) and PositionRank (Florescu and Caragea, 2017) introduced refinements to graph-based methods by incorporating topical and positional information. Despite their effectiveness, these traditional methods often struggle with capturing nuanced and contextual information, limiting their applicability in more complex scenarios. In recent years, embedding-based techniques have significantly advanced keyword extraction by leveraging dense vector representations of words and phrases. EmbedRank (Bennani-Smires et al., 2018), for instance, employs Word2Vec (Mikolov, 2013) and Sent2Vec (Pagliardini et al., 2017) to generate embeddings for candidate phrases, which are then ranked based on cosine similarity with the document's representation. Building on these foundations, more recent methods like PatternRank and KeyBERT have integrated contextual embeddings derived from advanced language models such as SBERT and BERT (Schopf et al., 2022; Grootendorst, 2020). These approaches also incorporate syntactic patterns, such as Part-of-speech (PoS) tagging, to refine candidate phrase selection and improve contextual relevance. While these methods represent a substantial shift towards contextual keyword extraction, their reliance on predefined patterns and embeddings highlights the need for further advancements, particularly in harnessing the capabilities of LLMs. In this regard, (Boudin and Aizawa, 2024) proposed SILK, an unsupervised domain adaptation method leveraging citation contexts to synthesize training data, addressing the scarcity of annotated in-domain keyphrases. Concurrently, (Wu et al., 2024) introduced MetaKP, a paradigm for on-demand keyphrase generation guided by user intents, combining supervised fine-tuning and LLM-based prompting to handle dynamic goals. These works collectively advance keyphrase generation using LLMs, demonstrating the field's shift toward flexible, resource-efficient solutions.

3 Dataset Construction

The multilingual dataset used for this study is constructed from the HAL database platform, an open archive dedicated to disseminating scientific research publications in French and English. Recent works, such as HALvest (Kulumba et al., 2024), demonstrate the underutilized potential of the HAL database for exploring and analyzing scientific publications. This dataset covers various scientific domains and its articles are accompanied by various information such as abstracts and author-provided keywords. We use abstracts, titles, and author-provided keywords, which will serve as a reference for evaluating the quality of the extraction methods. This dataset was compiled using a script that leveraged the HAL API. The collected data included approximately 12,000 articles. An initial sorting eliminated 1,300 duplicates, while about 6,000 other articles were excluded due to the absence of keywords or abstracts. After this filtering, the final corpus consists of 4,700 usable articles, representing about 30% of the initial data. An initial observation reveals a marked linguistic distribution with 85% of the articles in English and 15% in French. Regarding the English articles, the average number of keywords per article is 5.35, with an average keyword length of 2.14 words. In comparison, for French articles, the average number of keywords is slightly higher at 6.32, with an average length of 2.23 words.

The distribution of scientific domains also varies by language, as illustrated in Figure 2. Unsurprisingly, computer science remains the majority for both languages. Humanities rank second in French, while life sciences take this position in English. Humanities, well-represented in French, are less present in English. For the rest of the analysis, it is important to note that all titles, keywords, and abstracts were converted to lowercase to ensure consistent and reliable results.

4 Method

In this study, we approach keyword extraction through two distinct paradigms: *Generative Approaches* and *Embedding-Based Approaches*. For generative methods, we employ LLMs in a zero-shot learning framework, selected for its implementation simplicity and proven effectiveness in capturing baseline model performance. Formally, given an input document $D = \{w_1, ..., w_n\}$, the model generates candidate keywords K_G through conditional probability:

$$P(k|D) = \prod_{t=1}^{m} P(k_t|k_{<t}, D) \quad (1)$$

where $k \in K_G$ represents a generated keyword sequence of length m. The instruction prompt is a follows.

Instruction: *As a keyword extraction master, your only mission here is to extract only the most relevant keywords that are present in the text. Put the list of keywords between brackets, comma-separated. DO NOT write something else than the keywords you're supposed to extract from the text. Skip the preamble and provide only the keywords. The text:{text}*

The embedding-based approach operates by measuring semantic similarity between document embeddings $\mathbf{e}_D$ and keyword embeddings $\mathbf{e}_k$ from a predefined vocabulary $\mathcal{V}$, using cosine similarity. Keywords $K_E = \{k \in \mathcal{V} | \text{sim}(D, k) \geq \tau\}$ are selected through thresholding at τ. Our implementation leverages KeyBERT, a BERT-based framework that identifies document-subphrase alignment through this similarity measure. The system employs two distinct keyword selection strategies governed by:

Maximal Marginal Relevance (MMR) Balances keyword relevance and diversity through a trade-off parameter $\lambda \in [0, 1]$:

$$k_i = \arg\max_{k \in \mathcal{V} \setminus K_E} \Big[\lambda \cdot \text{sim}(D, k) - (1 - \lambda) \cdot \max_{k_j \in K_E} \text{sim}(k, k_j) \Big] \quad (2)$$

Max Sum Distance (MSum) : To diversify the results, it takes the 2 x top-n most similar words/phrases to the document. Then, it takes all top-n combinations from the 2 x top-n words and extract the combinations that are the least similar to each other by cosine similarity.

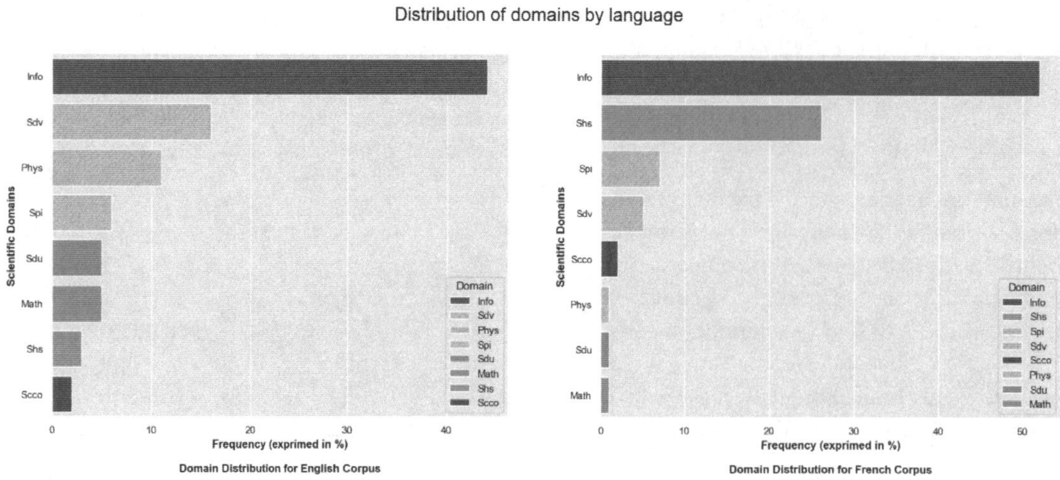

Figure 2: **Distribution of domains by language**

5 Experimental setup

In our study, we adopt an automatic evaluation framework to assess the performance of keyword extraction methods by comparing system-generated keywords against author-provided keywords from articles in the HAL open-access repository.

5.1 Methods

We evaluate three distinct categories of models. The first comprises multilingual LLMs that generate keywords in a generative manner, leveraging their pre-trained cross-lingual capabilities to produce contextually relevant terms. The second approach involves embedding-based models, where pre-trained embeddings encode textual content into dense vector representations, followed by clustering algorithms to identify salient keywords. The third category encompasses traditional statistical methods, which rely on frequency-based metrics, co-occurrence patterns, or graph centrality measures to extract candidate keywords.

Large Language Models The study leverages a diverse array of LLMs to ensure comprehensive evaluation across model architectures, scales, and accessibility frameworks. Open-weight models, chosen for their reproducibility and adaptability, include Meta's LLaMA 3.1 in both 70B and 8B parameter configurations, Mistral 7B, Mixtral 8x7B, and Google's Gemma 7B. These contrast with proprietary, closed-source models accessed via API, such as OpenAI's GPT-4o and GPT-3.5 Turbo, alongside Anthropic's Claude 3 Haiku and Claude Instant 1.2.

Embedding-based Models Our embedding-based approach employs KeyBERT, which utilizes pre-trained BERT embeddings to identify keywords by measuring semantic similarity between candidate terms and the input document. We evaluate two configurations: (1) a default setup relying solely on cosine similarity between document and keyword embeddings, and (2) an enhanced variant incorporating MMR for diversification and MSum to refine keyword selection by balancing relevance and novelty.

Traditional Models To establish robust baselines against contemporary neural approaches, we evaluate traditional unsupervised keyword extraction methods that rely on graph-based and statistical paradigms. This includes TextRank, a widely cited graph algorithm leveraging co-occurrence networks with PageRank-style scoring; PositionRank and SingleRank, which integrate term positional bias and heterogeneous graph structures, respectively; MultipartiteRank, optimized for topic-focused keyphrase extraction through multipartite graph representation; TopicRank, which hierarchically clusters candidate terms into topics before ranking; and YAKE, a lightweight statistical method combining term frequency, casing, and positional features.

5.2 Metrics

The comparison is performed within two approaches: **(1) Exact Matching**, where extracted keywords are evaluated based on their relevance

Model	Abstract + Title			Abstract		
	Precision	Recall	F1	Precision	Recall	F1
LLM-based Approach						
LLaMA 3.1 70b	0.132	0.245	**0.163**	0.120	0.224	**0.148**
Claude 3 Haiku	0.130	0.218	0.154	0.120	0.204	0.143
LLaMA 3.1 8b	0.147	0.181	0.151	0.136	0.172	0.142
GPT 4o	0.075	0.222	0.108	0.071	0.206	0.101
Claude Instant 1.2	0.073	0.183	0.097	0.066	0.171	0.088
GPT 3.5 Turbo	0.089	0.094	0.087	0.086	0.089	0.083
Mixtral 8x7b	0.057	0.188	0.083	0.047	0.176	0.070
Mistral 7b	0.050	0.199	0.077	0.048	0.156	0.069
Gemma 7b	0.051	0.079	0.059	0.052	0.081	0.060
Embedding-based Approach						
KeyBERT Default	0.058	0.081	0.067	0.056	0.078	0.065
KeyBERT with MMR and MSum	0.052	0.073	0.061	0.050	0.070	0.058
Traditional Approach						
PositionRank	0.062	0.115	0.080	0.056	0.103	0.072
MultipartiteRank	0.062	0.113	0.079	0.056	0.103	0.072
TopicRank	0.059	0.108	0.076	0.053	0.096	0.068
SingleRank	0.053	0.098	0.068	0.052	0.096	0.067
YAKE	0.053	0.098	0.068	0.045	0.083	0.058
TextRank	0.039	0.072	0.050	0.036	0.066	0.046

Table 1: **Evaluation Result with Exact Matching**

and precision compared to the keywords provided by the authors in their articles. The evaluation criteria include precision, recall, and the F1 measure. **(2) Fuzzy Matching**, which is a less strict method of term comparison without tolerance for variations such as plural forms, hyphen usage, or potential typographical errors.

Exact Matching In this approach, only identical terms were considered matches, to ensure a precise and consistent evaluation of the results. For each article, the most relevant keywords are extracted from the abstracts using all evaluated methods. We use the F1-Score, a commonly employed metric for evaluating the performance of keyword extraction models. The F1-Score is the harmonic mean between precision, which is the ratio of correctly extracted keywords to the total number of extracted keywords, and recall, which measures the proportion of relevant extracted keywords to the total number of relevant keywords in the text. In the context of keyword extraction, a high F1-Score indicates that the model successfully extracts a significant proportion of relevant keywords (high recall) while limiting the extraction of irrelevant keywords (high precision).

Fuzzy Matching This approach allows comparing generated keywords with reference keywords by considering formal variations. Several metrics can assign a "proximity score" between two strings, such as Levenshtein, Jaro-Winkler, and various embedding models (Alqahtani et al., 2021). In this study, we adopt the Levenshtein distance, also known as edit distance. It quantifies the minimum number of operations required to transform one string into another, with possible operations being insertion, deletion, or substitution of characters. The results are presented in graphical form to illustrate the evolution of the F1-Score as the flexibility of the Levenshtein distance increases (from 0 to 4).

6 Results

The evaluation results, as detailed in Table 1, compare model performance across precision, recall, and F1-score under two input settings: (1) Abstract With Title and (2) Abstract Only, ranked by decreas-

Model	Abstract + Title				Abstract			
	$d \leq 1$	$d \leq 2$	$d \leq 3$	$d \leq 4$	$d \leq 1$	$d \leq 2$	$d \leq 3$	$d \leq 4$
LLM-based Approach								
LLaMA 3.1 70b	**0.19**	**0.197**	**0.21**	**0.228**	**0.174**	**0.18**	**0.193**	**0.212**
Claude 3 Haiku	0.179	0.185	0.195	0.21	0.168	0.173	0.183	0.198
LLaMA 3.1 8b	0.175	0.183	0.198	0.223	0.165	0.172	0.187	0.21
GPT 4o	0.127	0.132	0.141	0.155	0.12	0.124	0.134	0.148
Claude Instant 1.2	0.116	0.13	0.147	0.176	0.105	0.118	0.135	0.163
GPT 3.5 Turbo	0.101	0.106	0.118	0.137	0.096	0.102	0.114	0.13
Mixtral 8x7b	0.1	0.107	0.118	0.133	0.084	0.095	0.107	0.123
Mistral 7b	0.092	0.097	0.107	0.123	0.085	0.09	0.099	0.116
Gemma 7b	0.069	0.072	0.076	0.084	0.071	0.073	0.078	0.086
Embedding-based Approach								
KeyBERT Default	0.084	0.095	0.12	0.158	0.081	0.092	0.116	0.154
KeyBERT with MMR and MSum	0.072	0.08	0.101	0.137	0.07	0.078	0.098	0.135
Traditional Approach								
PositionRank	0.097	0.101	0.108	0.123	0.087	0.091	0.099	0.114
MultipartiteRank	0.095	0.099	0.113	0.139	0.087	0.091	0.105	0.13
TopicRank	0.089	0.094	0.108	0.135	0.08	0.084	0.099	0.125
SingleRank	0.083	0.087	0.092	0.102	0.072	0.075	0.081	0.091
YAKE	0.081	0.085	0.094	0.113	0.079	0.082	0.091	0.11
TextRank	0.062	0.065	0.068	0.075	0.058	0.06	0.064	0.071

Table 2: **Evaluation Result with Fuzzy Matching (F1 Scores)**

ing effectiveness. Traditional graph-based methods exhibit stark disparities, with performance gaps exceeding 60% between the weakest (TextRank) and strongest models (PositionRank and MultipartiteRank). In contrast, KeyBERT demonstrates near-equivalent performance across both input variants, suggesting robustness to textual context. Notably, the inclusion of titles yields minimal impact on traditional and KeyBERT-based methods. However, LLMs display significant variability, with performance ranging from modest to triple-digit improvements when titles are included, boosting metrics by approximately 10%. The top-performing LLMs—LLaMA 3.1 70B, Claude 3 Haiku, and LLaMA 3.1 8B—highlight the role of scale and architecture in keyword extraction, while Gemma 7B's subpar performance underscores the criticality of prompt compliance, as deviations in output formatting led to severe penalties under exact-match evaluation.

The experimental findings, illustrated in Table 2, underscore the utility of Levenshtein distance in accommodating linguistic variations, which enhances precision at the cost of computational efficiency. While traditional models exhibit moderate performance gains when titles are included, KeyBERT demonstrates superior robustness in keyword extraction by leveraging contextual embeddings, particularly in texts with heterogeneous term distributions. This approach mitigates reliance on surface-level patterns, offering nuanced semantic alignment. LLMs, capitalizing on their deep contextual awareness and capacity to process structurally diverse texts, consistently outperform alternative methods, especially in complex extraction tasks. Generative architectures further benefit from the flexibility of Levenshtein-based evaluation, though title inclusion yields diminishing returns beyond a performance threshold. These results highlight a critical trade-off: while Levenshtein distance and contextual embeddings improve precision and adaptability, they introduce computational overhead. The interplay between model architecture, input context (e.g., title inclusion), and evaluation metrics emerges as a pivotal factor in optimizing keyword extraction systems, with LLMs setting a high benchmark for accuracy despite scalability challenges.

7 LLMs and Cost per Token

The computational and environmental costs of LLMs present critical barriers to accessibility and sustainability, particularly for institutions with limited resources. As evidenced by our analysis, models achieving comparable F1 scores can vary by 10–100x in operational costs per token, underscoring the need to integrate economic and ecological considerations into evaluation frameworks. To address this gap, we propose the Token Efficiency Score (TES), a novel metric balancing performance (F1) and cost ($/million tokens) through a weighted harmonic mean that prioritizes affordability without sacrificing accuracy. The formula,

$$\text{TES} = \frac{(1+\alpha) \times F_1 \times \text{Cost}}{\alpha \times \text{Cost} + F_1} \quad (\alpha = 10), \quad (3)$$

applies a strong penalty to cost, reflecting its outsized impact in mass data processing scenarios. While LLMs excel in task performance, their resource intensity highlights a critical trade-off: high-parameter models like GPT-4 achieve marginal gains at prohibitive expense, whereas smaller models (e.g., LLaMA-7B) offer viable efficiency-performance equilibria. TES not only democratizes model selection for resource-constrained environments but also incentivizes energy-conscious development, aligning AI progress with sustainability goals. This metric redefines evaluation paradigms, urging the community to prioritize computational equity alongside technical prowess—a crucial step toward ethical, scalable NLP solutions.

The calculation shows that the most performant models are also among the least costly, notably Llama-3 70B, Llama-3 8B, and Claude 3 Haiku. As shown in Figure 3, we rank the generative models by their TES score from most efficient to least efficient. As expected, the top three models are Llama 3 70B, Claude 3 Haiku, and Llama 3 8B, with Gemma 7B by Google in the last position. The TES allows for clear identification of the most performant models while considering the cost factor, which is crucial in large-scale scenarios.

8 Limitations

While LLMs have revolutionized keyword extraction through their contextual depth and adaptability, their deployment in scientific settings reveals critical limitations. First, their reliance on generic pretraining corpora restricts domain-specific precision, necessitating costly fine-tuning on annotated technical datasets to capture discipline-specific terminology. Second, their inherent opacity as "black-box" systems complicates interpretability, hindering traceability in scenarios requiring explainable keyword selection processes. Third, LLMs exhibit stochastic instability, with outputs fluctuating based on prompt phrasing—a challenge demanding iterative prompt engineering and repeated evaluations to stabilize F1-score performance. This instability is compounded by cost-efficiency trade-offs: verbose, conversational prompts may marginally improve keyword structure but inflate computational expenses without guaranteed gains in relevance. Finally, evaluation frameworks face intrinsic biases, exemplified by the HAL corpus, where absent keyword mentions in abstracts/titles disadvantage extractive models. These limitations underscore the need for domain-adapted training paradigms, standardized prompt templates, and evaluation corpora that align author-provided keywords with textual content—critical steps toward bridging the gap between LLM capabilities and scientific keyword extraction requirements.

9 Conclusion and Future Work

The experimental findings underscore the transformative potential of generative LLMs in keyword extraction, surpassing traditional methods in precision and semantic relevance, even in zero-shot settings. By capturing nuanced contextual relationships, LLMs produce keywords that better reflect scientific content, while our proposed Token Efficiency Score (TES) highlights cost-effective models—such as Claude 3 Haiku and LLaMA variants—that balance performance and affordability. Notably, integrating titles enhances F1-scores without significantly increasing computational overhead, emphasizing the value of metadata in extraction tasks. Future work should prioritize prompt engineering to stabilize outputs—for instance, by specifying keyword length or structuring prompts as simulated dialogues to reduce format variability, particularly for models like Gemma. Fine-tuning LLMs on domain-specific corpora could further bridge gaps between generative and extractive methods, while expanding processing to full-text articles (Teufel and Moens, 2002) promises

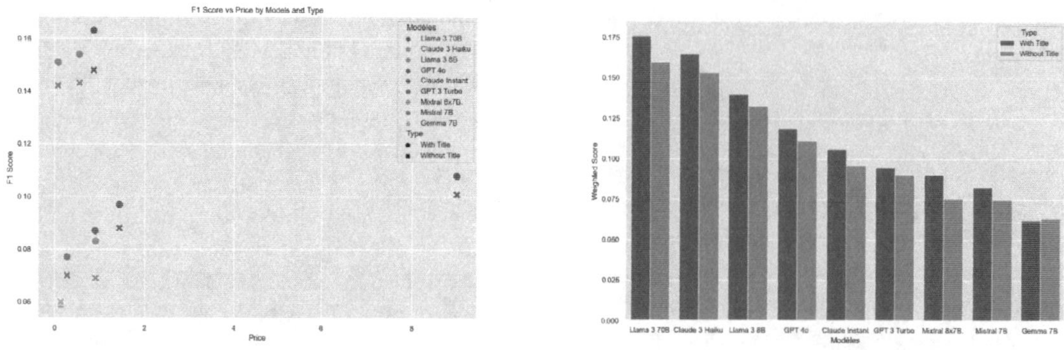

(a) F1 Score Performance relative to Price.

(b) Weighted Score

Figure 3: Cost and Weighted Score

richer keyword extraction by leveraging broader contextual signals. Complementing F1-score with metrics like NPMI and BM25 could better evaluate semantic coherence, and integrating thematic modeling (e.g., BERTopic) may organize keywords into structured taxonomies, enhancing interpretability. These directions not only refine extraction accuracy but also address scalability and domain adaptation challenges, laying the groundwork for LLMs to serve as versatile, sustainable tools for scholarly knowledge organization—a critical advancement as NLP increasingly intersects with scientific publishing and meta-research. This roadmap calls for interdisciplinary collaboration to align technical innovation with real-world usability and environmental responsibility.

Acknowledgment

We gratefully acknowledge the Sorbonne Center for Artificial Intelligence (SCAI) for partially funding this research.

References

Awatif Alqahtani, Hosam Alhakami, Tahani Alsubait, and Abdullah Baz. 2021. A survey of text matching techniques. *Engineering, Technology & Applied Science Research*, 11(1):6656–6661.

Kamil Bennani-Smires, Claudiu Musat, Andreea Hossmann, Michael Baeriswyl, and Martin Jaggi. 2018. Simple unsupervised keyphrase extraction using sentence embeddings. *arXiv preprint arXiv:1801.04470*.

Santosh Kumar Bharti and Korra Sathya Babu. 2017. Automatic keyword extraction for text summarization: A survey. *arXiv preprint arXiv:1704.03242*.

Florian Boudin. 2018. Unsupervised keyphrase extraction with multipartite graphs. *arXiv preprint arXiv:1803.08721*.

Florian Boudin and Akiko Aizawa. 2024. Unsupervised domain adaptation for keyphrase generation using citation contexts. *arXiv preprint arXiv:2409.13266*.

Adrien Bougouin, Florian Boudin, and Béatrice Daille. 2013. Topicrank: Graph-based topic ranking for keyphrase extraction. In *International joint conference on natural language processing (IJCNLP)*, pages 543–551.

David B Bracewell, Fuji Ren, and Shingo Kuriowa. 2005. Multilingual single document keyword extraction for information retrieval. In *2005 international conference on natural language processing and knowledge engineering*, pages 517–522. IEEE.

Ricardo Campos, Vítor Mangaravite, Arian Pasquali, Alípio Jorge, Célia Nunes, and Adam Jatowt. 2020. Yake! keyword extraction from single documents using multiple local features. *Information Sciences*, 509:257–289.

Samhaa R El-Beltagy and Ahmed Rafea. 2009. Kp-miner: A keyphrase extraction system for english and arabic documents. *Information systems*, 34(1):132–144.

Nazanin Firoozeh, Adeline Nazarenko, Fabrice Alizon, and Béatrice Daille. 2020. Keyword extraction: Issues and methods. *Natural Language Engineering*, 26(3):259–291.

Corina Florescu and Cornelia Caragea. 2017. Positionrank: An unsupervised approach to keyphrase extraction from scholarly documents. In *Proceedings of the 55th annual meeting of the association for computational linguistics (volume 1: long papers)*, pages 1105–1115.

Maarten Grootendorst. 2020. Bertopic: Leveraging bert and c-tf-idf to create easily interpretable topics. *Zenodo, Version v0*, 9(10.5281).

Fahrettin Horasan. 2021. Keyword extraction for search engine optimization using latent semantic analysis. *Politeknik Dergisi*, 24(2):473–479.

Daehoon Kim, Daeyong Kim, Eenjun Hwang, and Seungmin Rho. 2015. Twittertrends: a spatio-temporal trend detection and related keywords recommendation scheme. *Multimedia Systems*, 21:73–86.

Francis Kulumba, Wissam Antoun, Guillaume Vimont, and Laurent Romary. 2024. Harvesting textual and structured data from the hal publication repository. *arXiv preprint arXiv:2407.20595*.

Reza Yousefi Maragheh, Chenhao Fang, Charan Chand Irugu, Parth Parikh, Jason Cho, Jianpeng Xu, Saranyan Sukumar, Malay Patel, Evren Korpeoglu, Sushant Kumar, et al. 2023. Llm-take: Theme-aware keyword extraction using large language models. In *2023 IEEE International Conference on Big Data (BigData)*, pages 4318–4324. IEEE.

Rada Mihalcea and Paul Tarau. 2004. Textrank: Bringing order into text. In *Proceedings of the 2004 conference on empirical methods in natural language processing*, pages 404–411.

Tomas Mikolov. 2013. Efficient estimation of word representations in vector space. *arXiv preprint arXiv:1301.3781*, 3781.

Matteo Pagliardini, Prakhar Gupta, and Martin Jaggi. 2017. Unsupervised learning of sentence embeddings using compositional n-gram features. *arXiv preprint arXiv:1703.02507*.

Eirini Papagiannopoulou and Grigorios Tsoumakas. 2020. A review of keyphrase extraction. *Wiley Interdisciplinary Reviews: Data Mining and Knowledge Discovery*, 10(2):e1339.

Stuart Rose, Dave Engel, Nick Cramer, and Wendy Cowley. 2010. Automatic keyword extraction from individual documents. *Text mining: applications and theory*, pages 1–20.

Gerard Salton and Chris Buckley. 1990. A note on term weighting and text matching. Technical report, Cornell University.

Tim Schopf, Simon Klimek, and Florian Matthes. 2022. Patternrank: Leveraging pretrained language models and part of speech for unsupervised keyphrase extraction. *arXiv preprint arXiv:2210.05245*.

Mingyang Song, Yi Feng, and Liping Jing. 2023a. A survey on recent advances in keyphrase extraction from pre-trained language models. *Findings of the Association for Computational Linguistics: EACL 2023*, pages 2153–2164.

Mingyang Song, Xuelian Geng, Songfang Yao, Shilong Lu, Yi Feng, and Liping Jing. 2023b. Large language models as zero-shot keyphrase extractors: A preliminary empirical study. *arXiv preprint arXiv:2312.15156*.

Simone Teufel and Marc Moens. 2002. Summarizing scientific articles: experiments with relevance and rhetorical status. *Computational linguistics*, 28(4):409–445.

A Vaswani. 2017. Attention is all you need. *Advances in Neural Information Processing Systems*.

Xiaojun Wan and Jianguo Xiao. 2008. Single document keyphrase extraction using neighborhood knowledge. In *AAAI*, volume 8, pages 855–860.

Di Wu, Xiaoxian Shen, and Kai-Wei Chang. 2024. Metakp: On-demand keyphrase generation. *arXiv preprint arXiv:2407.00191*.

A Human-LLM Note-Taking System with Case-Based Reasoning as Framework for Scientific Discovery

Douglas B. Craig
Department of Emergency Medicine Research
Michigan Medicine, University of Michigan
Ann Arbor, Michigan USA
craigdou@med.umich.edu

Abstract

Scientific discovery is an iterative process that requires transparent reasoning, empirical validation, and structured problem-solving. This work presents a novel human-in-the-loop AI system that leverages case-based reasoning to facilitate structured scientific inquiry. The system is designed to be note-centric, using the Obsidian note-taking application as the primary interface where all components, including user inputs, system cases, and tool specifications, are represented as plain-text notes. This approach ensures that every step of the research process is visible, editable, and revisable by both the user and the AI. The system dynamically retrieves relevant cases from past experience, refines hypotheses, and structures research workflows in a transparent and iterative manner. The methodology is demonstrated through a case study investigating the role of TLR4 in sepsis, illustrating how the system supports problem framing, literature review, hypothesis formulation, and empirical validation. The results highlight the potential of AI-assisted scientific workflows to enhance research efficiency while preserving human oversight and interpretability.

1 Introduction

Large language models (LLMs) have the potential to transform scientific research. They offer broad domain knowledge and the ability to synthesize complex information. However, their application in scientific inquiry is hindered by issues such as hallucination, lack of transparency, and difficulty in tracing the reasoning process behind generated insights (Sanderson, 2023). To ensure that AI-driven research remains reliable, verifiable, and ethical, human-in-the-loop methodologies are essential.

Here we present a system that integrates case-based reasoning (CBR) (Kolodner, 1993; Watson, 1997) with a note-centric workflow to facilitate AI-assisted scientific inquiry. The system is designed around the Obsidian note-taking application (https://obsidian.md/) such that all elements of the workflow are represented as first-class plain-text notes in Obsidian. This structure provides a transparent, revisable, and interactive environment where users can inspect, modify, and refine the reasoning process at every stage.

The core workflow of the system follows a structured inquiry process. When a user poses a scientific question or problem, the system assesses whether it aligns with existing case knowledge and retrieves or adapts cases from prior solutions. Importantly, every step of a solution is documented within the note interface, including both user and LLM input, ensuring full traceability. Each step makes use of tools which can be called on explicitly, or searched for based on context.

We illustrate the potential of this approach through a case study exploring the role of TLR4[1] in sepsis. This example illustrates how the system facilitates problem framing, literature review, hypothesis generation, and data integration. The case study highlights the advantages of this structured, AI-augmented workflow.

2 Methods & Design

The system uses a human-in-the-loop approach that is note-centric. That is, all components of the system are stored as notes in the Obsidian note-taking application. All notes are plain-text documents. This includes not only user notes but all system CBR cases as well as tool specifications. This approach means that all elements of the system are transparently available to both the user and LLM as part of the workflow. This approach also means integration with the note-taking application is minimized making the system interface agnostic.

[1]Toll-like receptor 4 (TLR4) plays a central role in detecting bacterial infections. However, in some cases, it can trigger an excessive immune response, leading to sepsis.

Proceedings of the 1st Workshop on AI and Scientific Discovery: Directions and Opportunities, pages 22–30
May 3, 2025

This stands in contrast with fully integrated LLM-assisted note taking applications (Suh et al., 2023) (https://notebooklm.google/).

2.1 System Workflow

Figure 1 gives an overview of the system workflow. The user interacts with Obsidian, the note-taking application. While taking notes, the user may prompt the system to answer a question or solve a problem. The system evaluates the request and searches for any applicable CBR case. A new instance of the most similar case is then created and linked to from the current user note. If no case is found, a default case is created to initiate stepwise problem solving.

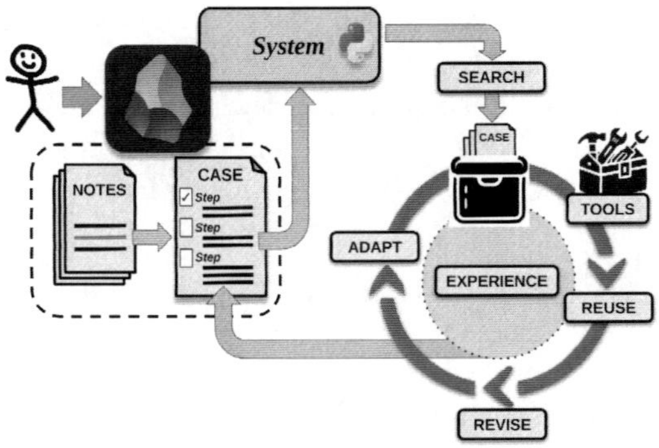

Figure 1: System workflow.

2.2 Case-based Reasoning

Case notes are structured documents that encapsulate knowledge for solving problems. Each case includes: a description of the problem, a series of steps for solving the problem and references to optional resources. Steps include an *Action* and may specify pre-conditions (*Requires*). The action is typically composed of a combination of free text instructions and references to system tools. When a tool is executed its response may be included inline in the note, or stored in a context variable. Variables may be passed to later steps. Abstractly, cases represent system experience based on previous problem solving instances. Cases may be reused, revised or adapted as new problems are encountered.

2.3 The Collaboration Process

After a case is instantiated and linked to the user's note the system begins execution of the steps. Because the case is a plain-text note, the user sees execution as it progresses. The user may pause execution to review, revise, and/or repeat steps. This keeps the user in-the-loop and makes the reasoning process interactive, transparent and traceable.

2.4 Language Enabled Tools

Tool usage and interface is specified in tool notes. As notes, this makes tools searchable both by the user and the system. This means that if a case step specifies some action, the system can search tool specifications for an appropriate tool to perform that action. Tools can also perform language functions (e.g., summarize) as well as retrieve or manipulate data (e.g., from user experiments) through a REST API. This also allows interface to any third-party database.

2.5 Implementation

The system is written in Python and interacts with the Obsidian note-taking application through notes written in plain-text markdown. For LLM-based tools Python interfaces to models (GPT4o and o1) through OpenAI's API (OpenAI, 2023). A Pinecone (https://www.pinecone.io/) serverless vector database maintains embeddings (text-embedding-ada-002 model) for all documents.

3 Case Study

Given that most available benchmarks assume significant autonomy/agency in performing knowledge discovery tasks (Liu et al., 2024; Majumder et al., 2024; Chen et al., 2024) or focus on a single correct/best answer (Rein et al., 2023; Chollet et al., 2025), we instead provide an end-to-end case study to demonstrate how a note-based system facilitates scientific inquiry through *collaboration with a user*. Specifically, the researcher initiates an exploration of how the TLR4 gene is related to sepsis. The approach supports an iterative framework that integrates user input, literature review, external database searches, hypothesis formulation and experimental results. Each step builds upon the previous, ensuring a well-documented and transparent reasoning path that is flexible, adaptable and supports a productive collaboration between human and machine.

3.1 Research Question

We begin by adding the following question to a new Obsidian note:

How is TLR4 related to sepsis?

The system must first contextualize the question/problem within the broader framework of scientific inquiry. This helps to set expectations for the nature of the insights and, more importantly, identify appropriate case-based reasoning (CBR) cases relevant to the question. A summary (Figure 2) is prepared by the *Note Change* case which assesses the original question.[2]

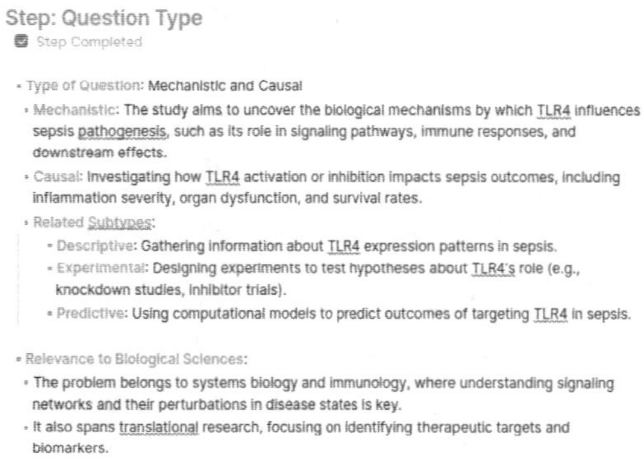

Figure 2: Defining the question type and identifying CBR cases (e.g., Mechanistic and Causal questions)

The user reviews the assessment, makes any needed changes and approves the summary (by checking "Step Completed"). This step will act as a guide for subsequent steps. That is, it informs and constrains subsequent step formulation as a part of any reasoning by the LLM. Note, especially, that this text is added to the original user note.

3.2 Initiating Case-based Reasoning

If available, an applicable "Question Type" case is chosen as a top-level starting point (if not, a "default" case formulates one). Here we have two main case types: mechanistic and causal, as well as three subtypes: descriptive, experimental and predictive. The original user note with question (and summary) will act as a top-level note with links to each subsequent reasoning step (Figure 3). The link is not to the Question Type case, but, rather, a copy which will be "populated" as each step in the case is completed and can be edited at any time by the user.

Note that steps in the following sections are specific to the above CBR case and, in fact, are only for the "Mechanistic" portion of the question as formulated in Figure 2. Though case specific, each step highlights features of the system available to

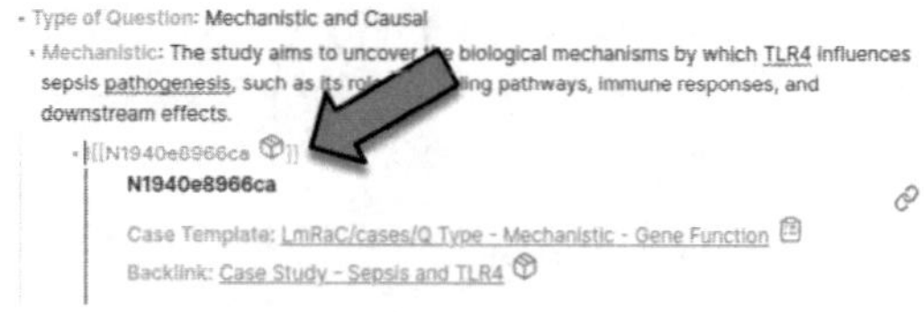

Figure 3: Instantiate intial CBR case, Mechanistic Gene Function, based on previous experience. Link this (red arrow) to the top-level user note.

any case.

3.3 Defining Scope

The first step of the 'Mechanistic - Gene Function' case is to define the scope of the problem. This requires user input. The step definition specifies this dependency in the *Requires* section with the instruction: "User input" (Figure 4). From what is known so far about the problem (which required user approval, see Figure 2) the LLM constructs a list of questions for gathering scoping information.

Figure 4: Case reasoning step requiring user input as part of the scope definition action.

Given the task of exploring a gene, this list (Figure 5) asks a series of questions designed to set bounds on what is to be investigated about that gene (e.g., species, interactions, relationship to disease).

Key to the system's collaborative design is that this is *not* a passive solicitation of information from the computer. Rather, the user may edit the list in any way, including using strikethrough to signal that items should be ignored. User answers are interleaved with questions and checkboxes are used to indicate the user has completed the question.

Given the user feedback, the Action portion of the step proceeds and the system proposes a working definition of scope (Figure 6). Again, the user may edit and revise as appropriate since all text is part of an Obsidian note. At this point the step is checked as completed and the next step begins.

3.4 Refining the Problem

We are now in a position to refine the original problem statement based on the agreed upon scope. In this step the Action implicitly uses the LLM to

[2]Note that most figure screenshots include red spell check underlines from Obsidian.

User Input
Here's a list of questions to gather additional input before defining the scope of the problem:

1. Focus and Depth
   - [x] Are you focusing on human studies, animal models, or both?
     - human only
   - [x] Should the analysis be limited to specific tissues or organs (e.g., lungs, liver, blood)?
     - no
   - [x] Do you want to prioritize any particular stage of sepsis (e.g., early, late, or recovery phase)?
     - early (presentation to emergency department)
2. Data and Literature
   - ignore this as part of the scoping step
   - [ ] ~~Do you already have access to any datasets, or do you want guidance on identifying relevant datasets (e.g., RNA-seq, proteomics, etc.)?~~
   - [ ] ~~Should the scope include a review of the latest clinical or experimental findings on TLR4?~~
3. Mechanisms and Pathways
   - [x] Are there specific pathways or signaling cascades (e.g., NF-κB, MAPK) that you want to prioritize in the analysis?
     - no
   - [x] Should the role of TLR4 be explored in both pro-inflammatory and anti-inflammatory responses?
     - focus on pro-inflammatory in sepsis
4. Integration with Other Factors
   - [x] Do you want to explore TLR4 interactions with specific co-factors or receptors (e.g., MD-2, CD14)?
     - not sure
   - [x] Should the analysis include the microbiota or other external factors influencing TLR4 activation?
     - yes, definitely
5. Sepsis Context
   - [x] Do you want to differentiate between the role of TLR4 in bacterial, fungal, or viral sepsis?
     - focus on bacterial
   - [x] Should the analysis explore the genetic polymorphisms of TLR4 and their association with sepsis outcomes?
     - no

Figure 5: Requested user information for scope definition. User interleaves answers and then checks boxes. Users may also use strike-through to indicate information that should be ignored (i.e., is out of scope).

Scope Definition
The study will focus on understanding the biological mechanisms by which TLR4 influences early sepsis pathogenesis in humans, particularly during the presentation to the emergency department. The analysis will explore the pro-inflammatory role of TLR4 in sepsis, focusing specifically on bacterial sepsis.

The study will not be limited to specific tissues or organs, aiming for a systemic perspective of TLR4 activation. It will include external factors such as the microbiota that influence TLR4 activation and their potential role in sepsis development. While the role of TLR4 interactions with specific co-factors or receptors (e.g., MD-2, CD14) remains uncertain, this may be considered if it emerges as critical during the investigation.

The scope excludes the exploration of genetic polymorphisms of TLR4 and downstream signaling pathways (e.g., NF-κB or MAPK), focusing instead on its broader pro-inflammatory activity and systemic impact during bacterial sepsis.

Figure 6: Final system composed question scope definition.

generate a Refined Problem Statement and propose Key Questions. The Step definition and results are both given in Figure 7.

Step: Refine Problem
- [x] Step Completed

Action
Using the question scope definition: refine the original problem statement to focus on a few key questions.

Refined Problem Statement
The study aims to uncover the biological mechanisms by which TLR4 influences early sepsis pathogenesis in humans, focusing on its pro-inflammatory role during bacterial sepsis. The analysis will explore systemic effects and external factors, such as the microbiota, that influence TLR4 activation at the time of emergency department presentation.

Key Questions:
1. How does TLR4 activation contribute to the systemic pro-inflammatory response observed in early bacterial sepsis?
2. What role do external factors, including the microbiota, play in modulating TLR4 activation during bacterial sepsis?
3. Are there specific mechanisms of TLR4-mediated inflammation that can be targeted to improve outcomes in early sepsis?
4. How does the timing and magnitude of TLR4 activation influence the progression of early bacterial sepsis, and what are the critical thresholds for transitioning from a controlled to a dysregulated immune response?

Figure 7: Refined problem statement and key questions. An additional question has been added by the user (blue highlight).

Notice that the user has exercised the option of adding an additional question (blue highlight). More generally, the system also fully supports not only editing responses, but also the Action definition itself. This serves two purposes, improving responses for a particular problem step, but also providing a mechanism for system learning. Since all case instances represent experience, any changes in how a problem is approached becomes an opportunity to refine and adapt CBR cases for future problems.

3.5 Quick Review

The adoption of LLMs for scientific research has been hindered by, among other things, their propensity to fabricate both information and citations supporting those fabrications (Jones, 2025). Nevertheless, their breadth of training can make them invaluable partners *if verification is included.*

In this step the LLM is used to provide a quick (though potentially unreliable) review of the problem. The Action uses an explicit system tool call to effect a search given the previously generated Problem Statement (Figure 8).

Step: Quick Review
- [ ] Step Completed

Action
Ask GPT for a review of the Refined Problem statement.
```
res0 = tool:GPTsearch({query})
{res0["answer"]}
```

Figure 8: Explicit tool call to ask OpenAI o1 model for "quick" non-authoritative answer.

By making the call explicit the return response can be captured in a named variable, *res0*. In doing so, the response will not be included as part of the note, however, by using a substitution statement after the tool, *{res0["answer"]}*, the response (aka answer) is both included in the note text (Figure 9) and now stored in a variable for later use (see 3.7 below).

1. How does TLR4 activation contribute to the systemic pro-inflammatory response observed in early bacterial sepsis?
TLR4 detects pathogen-associated molecular patterns—especially lipopolysaccharide from Gram-negative bacteria—triggering a cascade that rapidly amplifies the release of pro-inflammatory mediators (e.g., TNF-α, IL-1β, and IL-6). This surge in cytokines and chemokines mobilizes immune cells and activates endothelial pathways, leading to widespread vascular permeability, tissue injury, and the hallmark systemic inflammatory response of sepsis.

2. What role do external factors, including the microbiota, play in modulating TLR4 activation during bacterial sepsis?
The gut microbiota can prime or dampen TLR4-mediated responses by influencing baseline immune surveillance and shaping local inflammation in barrier sites. Changes in microbial composition or permeability (as in dysbiosis) can either heighten TLR4 signaling by exposing the host to more bacterial products or restrain it by promoting beneficial commensal interactions and regulatory immune pathways.

3. Are there specific mechanisms of TLR4-mediated inflammation that can be targeted to improve outcomes in early sepsis?
Targeting downstream signaling molecules, such as MyD88 and TRIF, or blocking TLR4 directly can modulate the excessive inflammation without fully compromising pathogen clearance. Novel therapeutic strategies also focus on interrupting the downstream cytokine storm or stabilizing the endothelium, aiming to reduce the deleterious effects of hyperinflammation while preserving essential immune defenses.

4. How does the timing and magnitude of TLR4 activation influence the progression of early bacterial sepsis, and what are the critical thresholds for transitioning from a controlled to a dysregulated immune response?
Early and balanced TLR4 engagement is crucial for effective pathogen recognition and clearance. However, if TLR4 is activated too robustly or persists beyond an initial window, the immune response can become dysregulated, shifting from protective to harmful. This tipping point often involves excessive cytokine release, endothelial dysfunction, and organ injury, signifying a transition from a contained inflammatory response to full-blown septic pathology.

Figure 9: "Quick" answers to the refined problem's key questions.

The LLM (OpenAI o1 in this case) answers each Key Question in a plausible, though unverified, manner. This step is meant to offer the user a quick overview as orientation to the problem space as well as prompt revision of earlier steps if the user believes this is appropriate (e.g., answers do not support a hypothesis the user has in mind).

3.6 Literature Review

With this cursory look at the answer in mind we may now undertake a more rigorous literature review. In this step the Action explicitly requests a search of PubMed articles to answer the Key Questions (Figure 10). Key to this tool is its design to explicitly *not* answer questions using the LLM. Instead, it collects articles based on a keyword search of PubMed (e.g., genes, diseases, pathways), indexes them and uses retrieval-augmented generation (RAG) to answer the questions (Lewis et al., 2020).

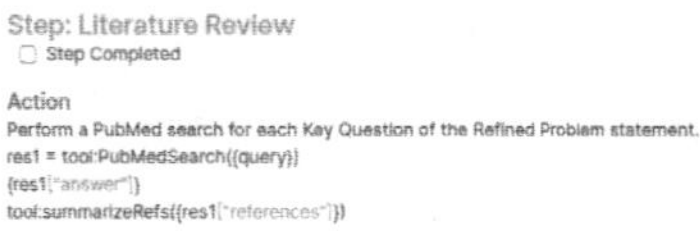

Figure 10: Initiate a literature search of PubMed on the list of Key Questions. Search results are stored in *res1* and references for search results are passed to another tool to be summarized.

Answers include paragraph-level citations to all articles used to answer the question as well as a complete linked bibliography (Figure 11).

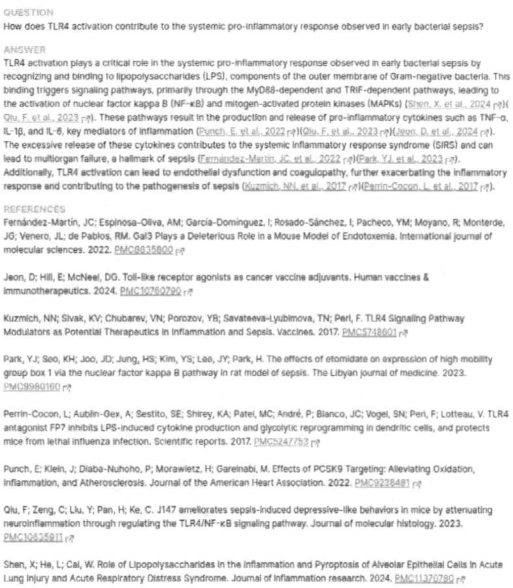

Figure 11: Literature Review answer to first Key Question. Answer is based *only* on PubMed articles with paragraph-level links to citations and bibliography (Fernández-Martín et al., 2022; Jeon et al., 2024; Kuzmich et al., 2017; Park et al., 2023; Perrin-Cocon et al., 2017; Punch et al., 2022; Qiu et al., 2023; Shen et al., 2024).

Though not shown here, the user has the option of revising any question, asking additional questions or otherwise annotating these results.

3.7 Knowledge Gaps

Having completed a first review of the Key Questions, we can now attempt to identify knowledge gaps that may warrant further investigation. This step (Figure 12) uses the same GPT tool as before but now incorporates information from previous steps (3.5 and 3.6) as part of the prompt using variable substitution (red arrows). It also explicitly specifies the structure of the response using a function prototype. Although this may border on "programming" for many users, it is shown here to demonstrate the level of control a user has over *how* the LLM answers questions.

Figure 12: GPT API is used to assess knowledge gaps. An explicit prompt is provided along with results from the previous Quick Review and Literature Review. The response is structured using a function prototype parameter.

The LLM, using both reviews, then provides a list of nine potential gaps in knowledge (Figure 13 shows the first two).

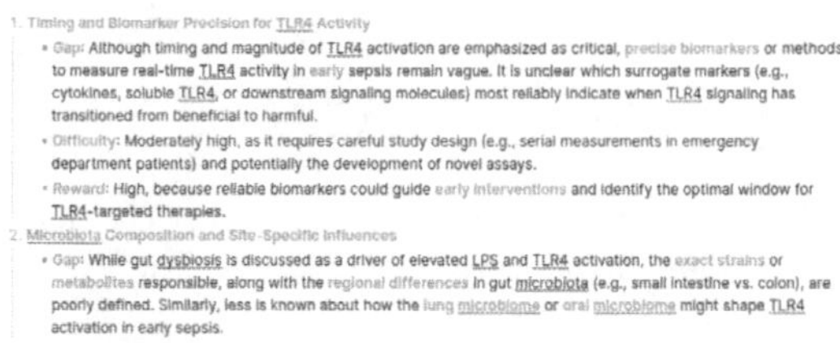

Figure 13: First two identified knowledge gaps (of nine) summarized and annotated by difficulty and reward.

Again, the strength of the LLM to identify and summarize is leveraged to provide a concise annotated summary of each potential gap. It remains up to the user to review, refine and approve the results. However, the system, by design, provides a documented, transparent path of reasoning steps to assist in this task.

3.8 Database Review

In addition to GPT and PubMed reviews, the user can also incorporate knowledge from other sources. This step (Figure 14) demonstrates the use of system tools to search, summarize and structure information from external sources, in this case: Wikipedia and GeneCards.

Step: Database Review
☐ Step Completed

Action
```
("dbList:["Wikipedia","GeneCards"])
res3 = tool:dbSearch("TLR4",{dbList})
{res3}
```

Wikipedia: TLR4

General Characteristics
- Name: Toll-like receptor 4 (TLR4), also known as CD284.
- Function: Activates innate immunity and plays a key role in bacterial infection defense.
- Structure: Transmembrane protein (~95 kDa) encoded by the TLR4 gene.
- Expression:
  - High in myeloid immune cells (e.g., monocytes, macrophages, dendritic cells).
  - Low in some non-immune cells (e.g., epithelium, endothelium, placental cells, Langerhans islet beta cells).

Activation and Ligands
- Recognizes pathogen-associated molecular patterns (PAMPs) such as lipopolysaccharides (LPS) from Gram-negative bacteria.
- Recognizes damage-associated molecular patterns (DAMPs) like HMGB1, S100 proteins, and histones, which are released during tissue damage or cell death.
- Facilitated by:
  - LPS-binding protein (LBP)
  - CD14
  - MD-2 protein (essential for receptor signaling).

Figure 14: Step definition to use two external data sources (Wikipedia and GeneCards) to summarize more information about the TLR4 gene.

The *dbSearch* tool takes a list of sources, queries them and then returns them to the user note. As before, these are added to the note, but also saved to a variable, *res3*, for later use by other functions.

3.9 Hypothesis Formulation

Given our Problem Statement; literature and database reviews; and, assessment of knowledge gaps, we can now attempt to formulate reasonable research hypotheses (Figure 15).

Step: Hypothesis Formulation
☐ Step Completed

Action
For the refined problem, formulate three hypotheses for further investigation using the above literature review, database review and knowledge gaps.

Figure 15: Using the results of multiple previous steps: formulate research hypotheses.

Reiterating: all work to this point has been recorded in a single user readable/editable note in Obsidian. It is available to the user, but also to the system. The Action in this step takes advantage of the accumulation of knowledge to formulate the hypotheses (Figure 16).

Three hypotheses are stated. The rationale for each is summarized and potential approaches for

Hypothesis 2: Gut Microbiota-Driven Modulation of TLR4

> Hypothesis
> **Dysbiosis** *of the gut microbiota—characterized by* ***specific strain imbalances*** *and elevated microbial-derived lipopolysaccharide (LPS)—****amplifies TLR4 signaling*** *in the early phase of bacterial sepsis, thereby* ***exacerbating systemic inflammation*** *and worsening patient outcomes.*

Rationale
- Directly tackles the gap on microbiota composition and site-specific influences (Gap #2).
- Integrates evidence that gut-derived LPS is a major activator of TLR4, with dysbiosis increasing intestinal permeability and systemic inflammatory responses.
- Extends current knowledge on how external factors, such as diet or the microbial environment, drive TLR4-mediated sepsis.

Potential Study Approach
1. Microbiome profiling (16S rRNA sequencing) of stool samples from sepsis patients at ED admission and 24 hours later.
2. Metabolomic analysis of short-chain fatty acids and other microbial byproducts known to influence TLR4 signaling.
3. Correlation of microbiota composition and metabolite levels with TLR4-associated biomarkers (e.g., NF-κB activation, IL-6 levels).
4. Interventional arm testing whether restoring gut microbiota balance (via targeted probiotics or fecal microbiota transplantation) reduces TLR4 hyperactivation and improves clinical outcomes.

Figure 16: Proposed Hypothesis 2, including: rationale and potential stepwise approach.

their study are given. This step in particular is a starting point. A user is expected to iterate and refine a hypothesis. This may mean qualifying or constraining a given hypothesis and re-running, or it may involve returning to earlier steps to gather more information (e.g., literature review). The use of a note taking system is meant to encourage and support the dynamic collaboration that is key to a scientific workflow.

3.10 Experiments and Data Collection

Another key feature of the system is the ability to seamlessly incorporate external data into reasoning tasks. In this case study the user has indicated an interest in Hypothesis 2 which integrates gut microbiota with changes in TLR4 signaling during sepsis (Figure 16). The Action has been edited by the user to focus data source search on this hypothesis (Figure 17).

Step: Experiments / Data Collection
☐ Step Completed

Action
What experiments or existing data sources would be useful for the proposed hypothesis number 2? Specifically, data that would potentially help provide some preliminary data for a larger project.

Figure 17: *Implicit* search of external resources for datasets suitable for preliminary results.

This search utilizes another section of the CBR case: *Suggested Resources* (Figure 18). This gives the system an *implicit* starting point for finding relevant data. Note that initially the databases are not themselves searched, but, rather, the LLM (OpenAI o1) utilizes its own training to locate possible sources. Like the GPT Literature Review (see 3.5) this is not meant to be a final authoritative search. Rather, it quickly locates possible data as well as giving guidance to the user (not shown) on how to search the database resources (e.g., GEO and SRA).

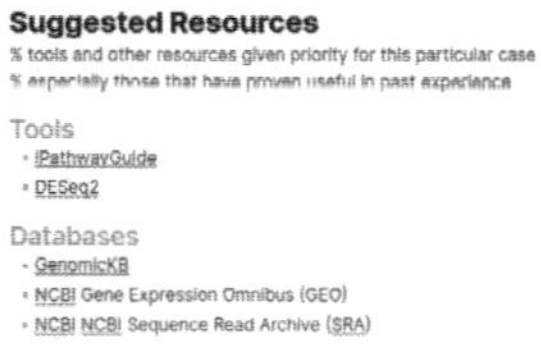

Figure 18: The CBR case includes Suggested Resources. This includes one for gene expression (GEO) and one for microbiome profiling (SRA).

Excerpted search results for both gene expression (from GEO) and microbiota profiling (SRA) are given in Figure 19. These results include accession identifiers (red arrows) as well as descriptions and relevance for Hypothesis 2 use.

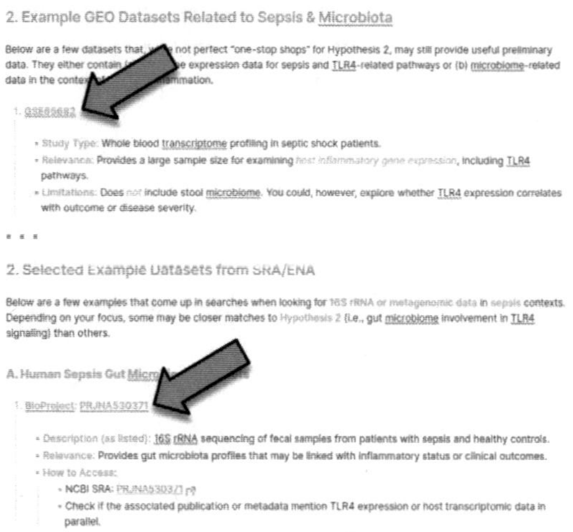

Figure 19: Excerpts from the search using OpenAI o1 model. Public datasets are identified (red arrows). Searches may also be done using tools to directly access resource APIs.

Again, this is meant as a way of using the LLM to quickly assess the availability of relevant public datasets. The user may then utilize other system tools (not shown) to search and download the actual data from GEO and SRA.

3.11 Differential Expression Analysis

Given that most data analysis, especially in the biological sciences, involves a multi-step pipeline, the advantages of initiating and monitoring a pipeline from a notes interface are limited. However, the system *does* have access, via its built-in REST API interface, for accessing the results of any analysis. What this means practically, is that these results can be incorporated into the workflow like any other text source.

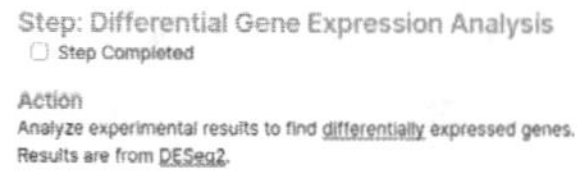

Figure 20: *Explicit* tool identification for computing differential gene expression on retrieved datasets.

Figure 20 implicitly calls a tool to interpret the results of a standard DESeq2 differential gene expression analysis. In this case the tool expects a list of genes in CSV format that includes: gene symbol (e.g., TLR4), log fold-change and significance of the change (typically, adjusted p-value). The results of the step are to summarize those genes that have been found to be significantly differentially expressed.

The user may then qualify these results relative to the workflow by posing additional questions (e.g., "Are other genes associated with an inflammatory response also up-regulated?").

3.12 Experimental Insights and Reflection

LLMs are particularly adept at summarization tasks. This CBR case takes advantage of this feature and asks the LLM in this final step to reflect on what has been discovered thus far and to suggest next steps (Figure 21).

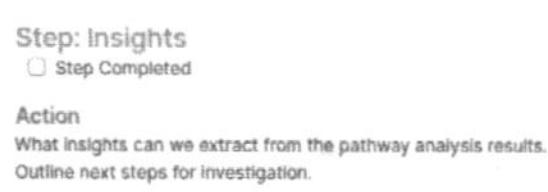

Figure 21: Preliminary results analysis and assessment of next steps sensitive to this analysis (if results are available).

Recall that each step has the accumulated context of all previous steps, so, although the Action may seem vague by asking for "insights," it is actually operating on the accumulated text of everything that has come before (nearly 20 pages in this case study).

In contrast to many autonomous reasoning systems (e.g., OpenAI's o1 model), this system is designed to support a scientific workflow that is *expected* to be open-ended and subject to continuous revision as hypotheses are generated and experiments are performed and interpreted. There is rarely, if ever, one right answer.

Figure 22 supports this workflow not only with a summary and critique of foregoing steps, but by giving guidance for refining and extending the work.

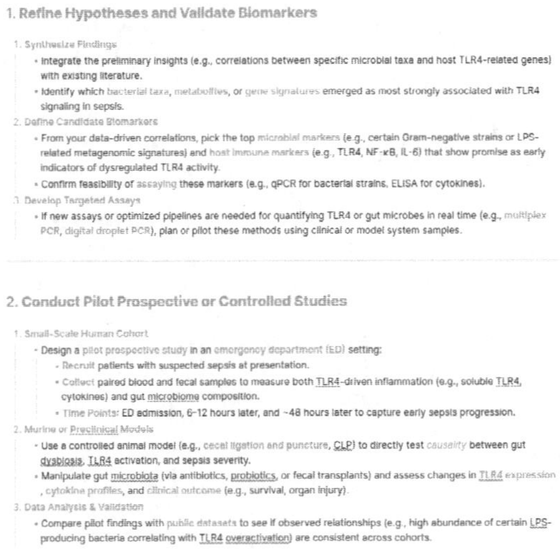

1. Refine Hypotheses and Validate Biomarkers

1. Synthesize Findings
   - Integrate the preliminary insights (e.g., correlations between specific microbial taxa and host TLR4-related genes) with existing literature.
   - Identify which bacterial taxa, metabolites, or gene signatures emerged as most strongly associated with TLR4 signaling in sepsis.
2. Define Candidate Biomarkers
   - From your data-driven correlations, pick the top microbial markers (e.g., certain Gram-negative strains or LPS-related metagenomic signatures) and host immune markers (e.g., TLR4, NF-κB, IL-6) that show promise as early indicators of dysregulated TLR4 activity.
   - Confirm feasibility of assaying these markers (e.g., qPCR for bacterial strains, ELISA for cytokines).
3. Develop Targeted Assays
   - If new assays or optimized pipelines are needed for quantifying TLR4 or gut microbes in real time (e.g., multiplex PCR, digital droplet PCR), plan or pilot these methods using clinical or model system samples.

2. Conduct Pilot Prospective or Controlled Studies

1. Small-Scale Human Cohort
   - Design a pilot prospective study in an emergency department (ED) setting:
     - Recruit patients with suspected sepsis at presentation.
     - Collect paired blood and fecal samples to measure both TLR4-driven inflammation (e.g., soluble TLR4, cytokines) and gut microbiome composition.
     - Time Points: ED admission, 6–12 hours later, and ~48 hours later to capture early sepsis progression.
2. Murine or Preclinical Models
   - Use a controlled animal model (e.g., cecal ligation and puncture, CLP) to directly test *causality* between gut dysbiosis, TLR4 activation, and sepsis severity.
   - Manipulate gut microbiota (via antibiotics, probiotics, or fecal transplants) and assess changes in TLR4 expression , cytokine profiles, and clinical outcome (e.g., survival, organ injury).
3. Data Analysis & Validation
   - Compare pilot findings with public datasets to see if observed relationships (e.g., high abundance of certain LPS-producing bacteria correlating with TLR4 overactivation) are consistent across cohorts.

Figure 22: First two (of six) suggested next steps for the investigation including, hypothesis refinement, validation and prospective controlled studies.

4 Discussion

The case study presented here illustrates how a human-in-the-loop AI system can enhance the process of scientific discovery. By structuring inquiry through case-based reasoning, the system provides a transparent, traceable, and iterative approach that naturally aligns with standard scientific workflows. A key strength of this approach is its ability to leverage LLMs as an integral tool for productive human collaboration.

A critical challenge in leveraging AI for scientific discovery is ensuring that the generated insights remain grounded in empirical evidence. LLMs are known to generate plausible yet unverified statements, which can mislead researchers if used uncritically. This system mitigates such risks by explicitly incorporating verification steps, including literature searches using PubMed and database reviews via other trusted sources. The interactive nature of the system ensures that the user remains an active partner in refining problem definitions, verifying outputs, and shaping hypotheses. This stands in stark contrast to many recent autonomous-blackbox approaches to LLM reasoning.

The foregoing case study demonstrates the value of structuring problem-solving through an evolving CBR system. Cases represent human-machine experience and as such can be reused, refined and adapted for new problems. Their implementation as first-class notes ensures transparency and encourages human collaboration as part of the reasoning process. In this example the iterative approach to scope definition, literature review, and hypothesis refinement steps serve as checkpoints, reinforcing scientific rigor while allowing for flexibility and refinement in inquiry. Using an LLM to help identify knowledge gaps and synthesize insights from multiple sources highlights the strength of this approach and demonstrates how AI can enhance, rather than replace, the natural reasoning process of scientific experts. Providing a mechanism for retrieving user experimental results further enhances the workflow by facilitating a seamless transition from hypothesis generation to empirical validation.

By embedding this approach within a human note-taking system, LLM-based tools become an integral component of the workflow, fostering a continuous cycle of learning and adaptation driven by user-machine collaboration. Furthermore, storing *all* CBR cases, tools, and generated results as user notes enhances transparency and traceability, ensuring that each step in the reasoning process remains accessible for review and refinement.

5 Conclusion

Our approach underscores the potential for human-in-the-loop AI systems to enhance scientific discovery by structuring inquiry, verifying insights, and integrating empirical data. By leveraging case-based reasoning, the approach ensures that LLM-generated outputs remain contextually relevant, empirically grounded, and are subject to a continuous step-by-step review by a collaborating human user.

The results demonstrate that while LLMs provide valuable breadth and summarization capabilities, their true scientific utility emerges when coupled with a human-in-the-loop. The interplay between user expertise and LLM-based tools creates a workflow that is not only transparent and accountable, but also adaptable to the evolving nature of all scientific inquiry. Ultimately, this approach represents a step toward AI-assisted research frameworks that align with the principles of scientific rigor and iterative discovery, paving the way for more effective collaboration between AI systems and domain experts in the pursuit of knowledge.

References

Ziru Chen, Shijie Chen, Yuting Ning, Qianheng Zhang, Boshi Wang, Botao Yu, Yifei Li, Zeyi Liao, Chen Wei, Zitong Lu, Vishal Dey, Mingyi Xue, Frazier N. Baker, Benjamin Burns, Daniel Adu-Ampratwum, Xuhui Huang, Xia Ning, Song Gao, Yu Su, and Huan Sun. 2024. ScienceAgentBench: Toward Rigorous Assessment of Language Agents for Data-Driven Scientific Discovery. *Preprint*, arXiv:2410.05080.

Francois Chollet, Mike Knoop, Gregory Kamradt, and Bryan Landers. 2025. ARC Prize 2024: Technical Report. *Preprint*, arXiv:2412.04604.

Juan Carlos Fernández-Martín, Ana María Espinosa-Oliva, Irene García-Domínguez, Isaac Rosado-Sánchez, Yolanda M. Pacheco, Rosario Moyano, José G. Monterde, José Luis Venero, and Rocío M. de Pablos. 2022. Gal3 Plays a Deleterious Role in a Mouse Model of Endotoxemia. *International Journal of Molecular Sciences*, 23(3):1170.

Donghwan Jeon, Ethan Hill, and Douglas G. McNeel. 2024. Toll-like receptor agonists as cancer vaccine adjuvants. *Human Vaccines & Immunotherapeutics*, 20(1):2297453.

Nicola Jones. 2025. AI hallucinations can't be stopped — but these techniques can limit their damage. *Nature*, 637(8047):778–780.

Janet Kolodner. 1993. *Case-Based Reasoning*. Morgan Kaufmann, San Mateo, CA.

Nikolay N. Kuzmich, Konstantin V. Sivak, Vladimir N. Chubarev, Yury B. Porozov, Tatiana N. Savateeva-Lyubimova, and Francesco Peri. 2017. TLR4 Signaling Pathway Modulators as Potential Therapeutics in Inflammation and Sepsis. *Vaccines*, 5(4):34.

Patrick Lewis, Ethan Perez, Aleksandra Piktus, Fabio Petroni, Vladimir Karpukhin, Naman Goyal, Heinrich Küttler, Mike Lewis, Wen-tau Yih, Tim Rocktäschel, Sebastian Riedel, and Douwe Kiela. 2020. Retrieval-Augmented Generation for Knowledge-Intensive NLP Tasks. In *Advances in Neural Information Processing Systems*, volume 33, pages 9459–9474. Curran Associates, Inc.

Xiao Liu, Zirui Wu, Xueqing Wu, Pan Lu, Kai-Wei Chang, and Yansong Feng. 2024. Are LLMs Capable of Data-based Statistical and Causal Reasoning? Benchmarking Advanced Quantitative Reasoning with Data. *Preprint*, arXiv:2402.17644.

Bodhisattwa Prasad Majumder, Harshit Surana, Dhruv Agarwal, Bhavana Dalvi Mishra, Abhijeetsingh Meena, Aryan Prakhar, Tirth Vora, Tushar Khot, Ashish Sabharwal, and Peter Clark. 2024. Discovery-Bench: Towards Data-Driven Discovery with Large Language Models. *Preprint*, arXiv:2407.01725.

OpenAI. 2023. GPT-4 Technical Report. *Preprint*, arXiv:2303.08774.

Yoo Jung Park, Kwon Hui Seo, Jin Deok Joo, Hong Soo Jung, Yong Shin Kim, Ji Yung Lee, and Hunwoo Park. 2023. The effects of etomidate on expression of high mobility group box 1 via the nuclear factor kappa B pathway in rat model of sepsis. *The Libyan Journal of Medicine*, 18(1):2182683.

Laure Perrin-Cocon, Anne Aublin-Gex, Stefania E. Sestito, Kari Ann Shirey, Mira C. Patel, Patrice André, Jorge C. Blanco, Stefanie N. Vogel, Francesco Peri, and Vincent Lotteau. 2017. TLR4 antagonist FP7 inhibits LPS-induced cytokine production and glycolytic reprogramming in dendritic cells, and protects mice from lethal influenza infection. *Scientific Reports*, 7:40791.

Emily Punch, Justus Klein, Patrick Diaba-Nuhoho, Henning Morawietz, and Mahdi Garelnabi. 2022. Effects of PCSK9 Targeting: Alleviating Oxidation, Inflammation, and Atherosclerosis. *Journal of the American Heart Association: Cardiovascular and Cerebrovascular Disease*, 11(3):e023328.

Fang Qiu, Changchun Zeng, Yuqiang Liu, Haobo Pan, and Changneng Ke. 2023. J147 ameliorates sepsis-induced depressive-like behaviors in mice by attenuating neuroinflammation through regulating the TLR4/NF-KB signaling pathway. *Journal of Molecular Histology*, 54(6):725–738.

David Rein, Betty Li Hou, Asa Cooper Stickland, Jackson Petty, Richard Yuanzhe Pang, Julien Dirani, Julian Michael, and Samuel R. Bowman. 2023. GPQA: A Graduate-Level Google-Proof Q&A Benchmark. *Preprint*, arXiv:2311.12022.

Katharine Sanderson. 2023. GPT-4 is here: What scientists think. *Nature*, 615(7954):773–773.

Xiao Shen, Linglin He, and Wanru Cai. 2024. Role of Lipopolysaccharides in the Inflammation and Pyroptosis of Alveolar Epithelial Cells in Acute Lung Injury and Acute Respiratory Distress Syndrome. *Journal of Inflammation Research*, 17:5855–5869.

Sangho Suh, Bryan Min, Srishti Palani, and Haijun Xia. 2023. Sensecape: Enabling Multilevel Exploration and Sensemaking with Large Language Models. In *Proceedings of the 36th Annual ACM Symposium on User Interface Software and Technology*, pages 1–18, San Francisco CA USA. ACM.

Ian Watson. 1997. *Applying Case-Based Reasoning: Techniques for Enterprise Systems*, 1st edition edition. Morgan Kaufmann, San Francisco, Calif.

Towards AI-assisted Academic Writing

Daniel J. Liebling†[1], Malcolm Kane*[1], Madeleine Grunde-Mclaughlin[2], Ian J. Lang‡[1], Subhashini Venugopalan*[1], and Michael P. Brenner‡[1]

[1]Google Research, †Seattle | *Mountain View | ‡Cambridge, USA
[2]Paul G. Allen School of Computer Science & Engineering, University of Washington, Seattle, WA, USA

Abstract

We present components of an AI-assisted academic writing system including citation recommendation and introduction writing. The system recommends citations by considering the user's current document context to provide relevant suggestions. It generates introductions in a structured fashion, situating the contributions of the research relative to prior work. We demonstrate the effectiveness of the components through quantitative evaluations. Finally, the paper presents qualitative research exploring how researchers incorporate citations into their writing workflows. Our findings indicate that there is demand for precise AI-assisted writing systems and simple, effective methods for meeting those needs.

1 Introduction

Scientific communication, including writing, is a necessary professional skill set. For example, The American Chemical Society guidelines for undergraduate education indicate that students must "learn how to communicate technical information ... clearly and concisely, [i]n a scientifically appropriate style"' (American Chemical Society). Writing effective prose is a skill developed through practice and feedback. Although the vast majority of scholarly publications are written in English, most English-language authors are not L1 English speakers. The proficiency gap negatively affects productivity of non-L1 authors. For example, Flowerdew (1999) found that over two-thirds of L1 Cantonese academic authors, writing in English, felt disadvantaged relative to L1 English speakers. Even for L1 speakers, the precise nature of scholarly language takes time and practice to develop expertise. Morris (2023) interviewed scientists, who noted that their students were often "not strong writers." The respondents anticipated that assisted writing would "improve writing quality for a large number of students."

Writing is fundamentally a task of translating ideas into text (Flower and Hayes, 1981). Interactive writing systems guide authors through the writing process by destructuring the writing process and, most recently, generating fluent language. Borrowing from crowdsourcing, *Play Write* (Iqbal et al., 2018) "selfsourced" writing tasks through microtasks divorced from the document editor and delivered to the end user by an app. The tasks included outputs of typical NLP tasks such as summarization and grammar correction. Whereas older systems delegated tasks to the individual or crowd works, recent works incorporate LLMs as user-guided co-creators. For example, *Wordcraft* (Yuan et al., 2022) focused on story writing. The system provided affordances for rewriting, elaborating, and open text generation. *Sparks* (Gero et al., 2022a,b) used a LLM to suggest starter sentences intended to catalyze creative, compact writing for a general audience. Similar to users of Wordcraft, users of Sparks found value simply in generating narrative.

Computer-assisted writing is not a new concept; among others, Mahlow (2023) notes that AI-assisted writing is already commonplace. Modern LLMs are capable of generating text in scientific contexts comparable to expert human authors (e.g. Wang et al. (2019); Ali et al. (2023); Gao et al. (2023a)) although this depends on the context (c.f. Ruggeri et al. (2023)). Scientifically-grounded text generation is part of a larger adoption of AI in the sciences (Hope et al., 2022). In this paper, we present two affordances for generative text in scientific contexts: citation recommendation and introduction writing. We develop and evaluate these affordances in the context of user-facing AI-assisted writing. Finally, we present the results of qualitative research on how researchers incorporate citation recommendations into their workflows. The system and findings show that AI-assisted writing is capable of generating useful content for aca-

Proceedings of the 1st Workshop on AI and Scientific Discovery: Directions and Opportunities, pages 31–45
May 3, 2025

demic authors, and that richer *in situ* affordances can provide users with agency to craft more precise scholarly manuscripts.

2 Contextual citation recommendation

The citation recommendation task is typically framed as a recommender system that produces a ranked list of possible citations. Various approaches developed over time as machine learning methods evolved. Färber and Jatowt (2020) provide an overview of techniques that predate large language models (LLMs). Most techniques encode academic works into some semantic similarity (e.g. a topic model (Kataria et al., 2010) or an embedding (Beltagy et al., 2019)). Graph-based approaches (Ali et al., 2024) use the directed graph of citations as features or as a network for propagation of existing features.

Locating, copying, and formatting citations to include in the project takes time and effort. When performed concomitantly with writing, this context-switch between citation discovery can interrupt the user's writing flow.

We imagine *in situ* citation recommendation as a task which recommends citations given the user's context and focus. Here, the focus is the cursor (insertion point) in the active document, representing the desired location of the suggestion. The context is some substring of the document leading up to the insertion point. We envisioned multiple scenarios for suggestions, depending on how much context the author has, and what type of output they desire. Consider the known-item refinding task where the author knows of a specific work and wishes to cite it. Frequently, the author can recall details about the work that they wish to cite (Wildemuth and O'Neill, 1995; Bruce et al., 2004), although the known details might be incorrect. The author might recall these with a lower degree of precision (i.e. "about 5–10 years ago" or "at an NLP conference" or "from Yamada Hanako's lab"). Finally, the author might not recall any of the indexing details of the paper. Instead they might remember a summary of the contribution. These incomplete or incorrect semantic cues to the underlying item are opportunities for the system to use additional context and world knowledge for recommending citations.

2.1 Implementation

Our system recommends citations from two sources. First, a user's writing project typically contains one or more files with citations expressed as structured content, e.g. BibTeX. Second, the system contains a local database of scholarly works: a copy of the OpenAlex corpus (Priem et al., 2022). Each record in this corpus includes the work's author(s), title, abstract, date, publication venue, citation count, and so forth. We used a language detection classifier to exclude works that appeared to be written in a language other than English. Because the mode of citation count is zero, we also excluded uncited works. Since the experiments documented herein were performed, the current implementation of the system retains recent uncited works in the database to allow them to be surfaced. After filtering, our database copy had 60.3 million rows out of the original 263.3 million rows.

As an interactive system, reducing response latency is critical to user perception and satisfaction. The system uses a highly scalable approximate nearest neighbor search (Sun et al., 2024) index for rapid retrieval of similar records in an embedding space. We chose the SPECTER2 embedding (Singh et al., 2023), a multi-format embedding developed specifically to represent scientific documents. SPECTER2 was trained on data from 23 different fields, not limited to computer science. SPECTER2 embeddings outperformed existing models on retrieval tasks. Our system concatenates each paper's title and abstract (if available in the OpenAlex record), projecting this text into the SPECTER2 embedding space.

In addition to works available within the user's BibTeX files, the system needs to find novel candidates from the index that satisfy the user's intent. We implement this recommender as a Retrieval Augmented Generation (RAG) system (Gao et al., 2023b). To retrieve a set of relevant citations, the system queries the index of existing works. Recall that the works are represented by a vector embedding of the title and abstract. The system takes advantage of LLMs observed behavior of "hallucinating" nonexistent facts or concepts (Ji et al., 2023). Essentially, we prompt the LLM to fabricate a likely citation and then use that to find real citations. To do this, the system supplies the LLM with a prompt (see Appendix A.1) containing the previous, current, and subsequent sentences from the user's content. The current sentence contains a special token which indicates to the system where in the sentence the citation is desired. The prompt instructs the LLM to fabricate the title and abstract of a paper that satisfies the user's context. Note that the system does not care if the LLM's generated citation exists. Rather, the fabricated citations are used as queries into the index of existing works. The fabricated title and abstract are embedded using the SPECTER2 model, which creates a vector used to query the nearest-neighbor index. As implemented, at most 10 nearest neighbors are returned.

Although each result could be ranked by its distance to the query vector in embedding space, we apply an additional layer of scoring. Each result retrieved from the index is formatted into a new prompt (Appendix A.2. These results are formatted as JSON objects. Each result is also given a unique, short hexadecimal string as a "key" property. Keys are constructed rather than using ordinal numbers (1, 2, ...) or letters (A, B, ...) to avoid label bias (Reif and Schwartz, 2024). Some LLMs also exhibit order bias (Shi et al., 2024); we did not evaluate this in our study. The prompt instructs the LLM to output the key that matches "best citation to support [the] claim." Rather than using the key as output, the system runs model inference and collects the model's *scores* for each of the keys in the input. A model's output score for each key is, to an approximation, the log probability of outputting that key to complete the input (prompt). The results are then ranked by their respective scores. Prompt inference was only run once for each item; no additional sampling of LLM output was performed.

We also implemented pairwise comparison to score suggestions. Qin et al. (2024) showed that LLMs can be used to rank by presenting pairwise choices and having the LLM choose one of the items. This method differs from the scoring method described above. The model is prompted to choose the item from a pair of items that best matches the prompt. By combining pairwise ranks, one can determine a total ranking. By focusing the model's attention on a smaller number of targets, adverse effects from irrelevant targets are avoided.[1] Constructing the total ordering requires many pairwise comparisons. Although some techniques for reducing the quantity of comparisons exist (Bradley and Terry, 1952; Chen et al., 2013), we discarded this method due to the substantial increase in inference time, favoring the scoring method above.

The online citation recommender system allows the user to request a set of citation suggestions by right-clicking in the text editor. The client sends a substring of text adjacent to the insertion point, as well as the contents of BibTeX files. The latter include structured data about publications the author intends to cite.

2.2 Evaluation

To assess the efficacy of our citation recommendation system, we evaluated the LLM's performance on the task of retrieving ground truth citations extracted from existing papers. The evaluation dataset was created from papers in S2ORC, a corpus of over 81 million papers spanning STEM disciplines (Lo et al., 2020). We uniformly sampled 0.1% of papers from this corpus, then filtered to papers that include at least 10 sentences that include citations that existed in OpenAlex prior to September 2023 (our cutoff date). This ensured that the system would have access to titles and abstracts for these citations and would be able to use them as distractors in our evaluations. Five citation-containing sentences were randomly sampled from each qualifying paper, resulting in a dataset of 1015 sentences.

For each sentence, we gathered the necessary inputs to run the suggestion citation prompt described in Section 2.1. This includes the target sentence's surrounding context and titles and abstracts of n possible citations, for $n \in \{3, 5, 10\}$.

The n candidate citations included the ground truth citation and $n - 1$ distractor citations. We chose distractors in three different ways to test the system under varying difficulty. From least to most difficult, distractors were chosen uniformly randomly from:

- all papers in the evaluation dataset (sample of S2ORC)
- the ground-truth citation's nearest neighbors in SPECTER2 embedding space
- the references of the source paper containing the test sentence, excluding the ground truth reference

We employ Precision at *k* (P@k) and mean reciprocal rank (MRR) as evaluation metrics. Because the randomly chosen set of distractors is domain agnostic, we expect a paper chosen from S2ORC at random to be unrelated to the test sentence. The two more difficult distractor sources include papers that are semantically related. In the *nearest neighbors* condition, one of the distractors could be a reasonable substitute for the ground truth citation, particularly for well-known results.

[1] c.f. Cuconasu et al. (2024), where noise improves quality.

Distractor Type	n	MRR	$p@1$	$p@3$	$p@5$
Random	3	0.755	0.612		
Random	5	0.549	0.333	0.665	
Random	10	0.320	0.124	0.348	0.500
Nearest neighbors	3	0.661	0.428		
Nearest neighbors	5	0.506	0.254	0.661	
Nearest neighbors	10	0.300	0.110	0.327	0.523
References	3	0.676	0.462		
References	5	0.496	0.261	0.641	
References	10	0.308	0.109	0.326	0.519

Table 1: Retrieval metrics for 1,015 contextual citation retrieval cases with n targets.

Table 1 shows the results. As expected, the ground truth citation tends to rank higher against randomly selected distractors when compared to distractors drawn from the semantic space or from the manuscript's references. However, the distractor source has less effect on precision. In a live system that uses this method, the user would need to choose from multiple suggestions rather than having the system propose only the top-ranked item.

3 Writing introductions

3.1 Generating introductions

We frame the introduction writing task as a mapping from the manuscript and references to a small number of paragraphs. The related work in the introduction should act like a microscope: canonical works coarsely orient the reader to a subfield; important recent works provide fine adjustment to the specific research track. Upon this foundation, the introduction builds the case for the specific contribution of the manuscript that follows. Our prompt chain follows this paradigm in three steps.

First, the system uses an LLM to identify novel claims from the author's manuscript relative to other works that the author cited. It assumes that the author already documented references in their BibTeX files at this time. For each reference, the system looks up the corresponding record in the OpenAlex database, retaining only those where a title and abstract are available. These references are split into two groups: *canonical* and *recent*. The *canonical* references were published more than Y years ago while *recent* were published within the last Y years. As in other systems, our system uses the title and abstract as a rough substitute for the work itself (Li and Ouyang, 2024). To perform the relative comparison, the system then extracts paragraphs from the author's current work. Each paragraph is then combined with each of the references to form tuples of (paragraph, title, abstract). The prompt (Appendix B.1) acts as a binary classifier that confounds relevance and novelty. The LLM assess if the each paragraph's content is related to the abstract of the author's paper *and* it is novel relative to the abstract a cited paper. The idea is to use this filter to find the work's novel contributions for incorporation into the introduction.

Each paragraph then receives one or more votes from the binary classifier. The system filters out paragraphs with low support. The remaining paragraphs, assumed to discuss novel results, are then passed to a simple summarization prompt (Appendix B.2. Although current LLMs have long context lengths, at the time of our experiments, the token limit was smaller, and hence the (possibly many) novel paragraphs needed to be reduced into a shorter text.

Finally, the system combines the canonical works, recent works, and summary of novel contributions into the written introduction section using the prompt in Appendix B.3. Example output of running the prompt chain on this submission is provided in Appendix C.

3.2 Evaluation

We evaluate the generated introductions using text metrics and by prompting an LLM. Our evaluation dataset is a subset of papers from the [United States] National Bureau of Economic Research[2] (NBER). We extracted the introduction from 14 NBERs papers. For text evaluations, we use ROUGE (Lin, 2004) which is a recall-based metric and often used in the context of summarization.

[2]https://www.nber.org/research/data

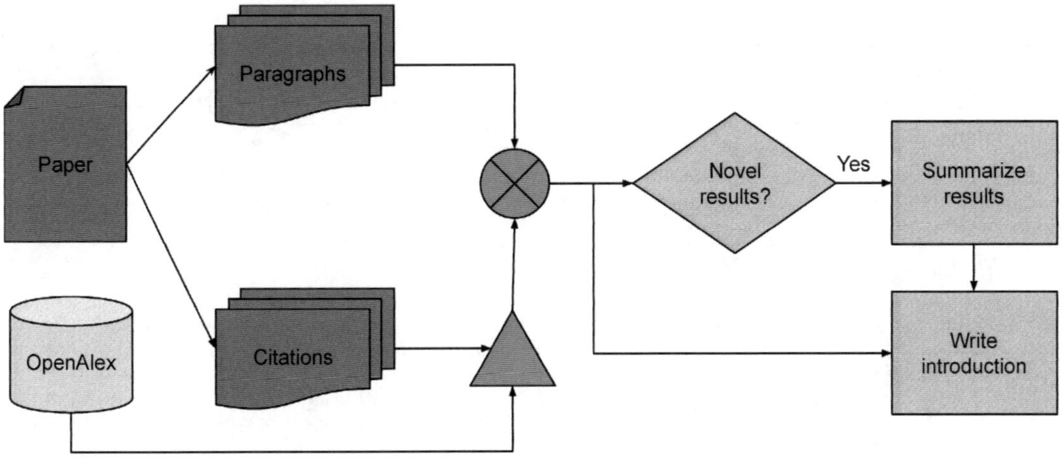

Figure 1: Flowchart from paper and citations to written introduction.

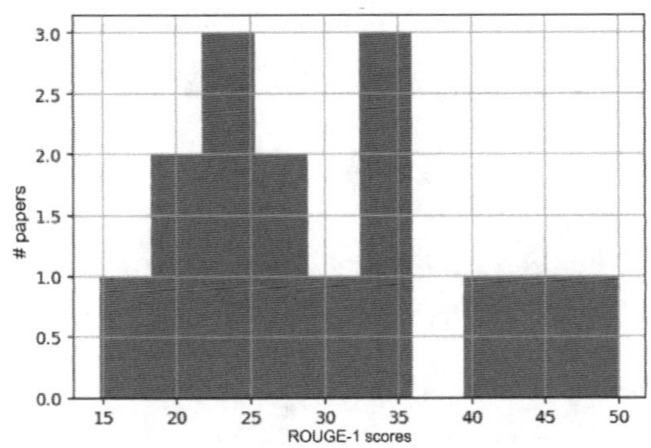

Figure 2: Distribution of ROUGE-1 scores for the generated introductions.

The average ROUGE score across the papers is 29.9, the distribution of scores is shown in Figure 2.

For LLM-based evaluations, we consider evaluating the introductions based on the claims made in the generated introductions in comparison to the original introductions. Specifically, we used a prompt (Appendix B.4) to extract 3–5 claims from each of the generated texts. From 14 generated introductions, we extracted 52 claims. Then, we prompt the LLM to verify whether the claim from the generated introduction entails from the full original introduction. Appendix B.5 includes the full prompt used. We consider two versions of the LLM based evaluation: (1) we ask the LLM for a simple "yes" or "no" response for the prompt, (2) we consider the log-likelihood scores for the "yes" and "no" response tokens and normalize them to determine the probability that the generated claim is entailed from the the original. Figure 3 presents the probability scores for whether claims from the generated introduction entail from the original introduction. Of the 52 claims extracted from the generated introductions, 47 of them are entailed from the original introduction indicating a high degree of precision. In general, we find that the generated introductions score highly when the original introduction section hews closely to a single topic. Table 2 compares a generated paragraph from NBER 20209 (Borovička et al., 2014) with entailment score 0.983 versus a lower-performing paragraph from NBER 22392 (Nakamura et al., 2016) with entailment score 0.279. The higher-scoring generated passage captures the main concepts from the original work, while the lower-scoring passage hones in on natural disasters, which is not the theme of the original work. The LLM correctly identified the paragraph as not entailing the original. It seems reasonable to expect that self-critique (Madaan et al., 2023) can be used to improve generated introductions in the future.

4 Opportunities

As part of a study on citation verification, we conducted semi-structured interviews with academic authors about their experiences citing related work. Six researchers (5 self-identifying as men; 1 woman) from the research division of a large technology company participated. All researchers are experienced academic authors (mean h-index 26, $\sigma = 13$). Their research domains include subfields of computer science including quantum computing, virtual reality, biomedical imaging, natural language processing, and responsible artificial intel-

Original excerpt	Generated excerpt
NBER 20209, entailment 0.983	
It has been known, at least since the path-breaking work of Arrow, that asset prices reflect a combination of stochastic discounting and probability distributions. ... We demonstrate in Section 5 that a Perron–Frobenius approach leads naturally to the construction of a martingale component ...	This research explores alternative solutions by investigating the application of Perron–Frobenius theory to construct a probability distribution from Arrow prices. ...
NBER 22392, entailment 0.279	
However, just because the inhabitants of some locations have higher incomes than others does not mean there is a large causal effect of moving to these locations. ... Distinguishing between selection and direct causal effects of locations is challenging. Large, exogenous relocation shocks are few and far between ... We shed new light on the role of location in shaping economic outcomes by studying the consequences of a true "natural" experiment. On January 23, 1973, a long-dormant volcano erupted unexpectedly on the Westman Islands ...	The impact of natural disasters on economic development is a topic of considerable interest to economists. While the immediate consequences of natural disasters are often well documented, the long-term impacts are less well understood. In particular, the impact on intergenerational mobility and the transmission of risk across generations is a critical yet underexplored area of research. <cit.> have shown that children who spend more time in a low-poverty environment have better long-term outcomes. This suggests that the effects of natural disasters may not only be felt by those who experience them directly, but also by future generations.

Table 2: Comparison of two generated introduction paragraphs with high and low entailment scores relative to the original text.

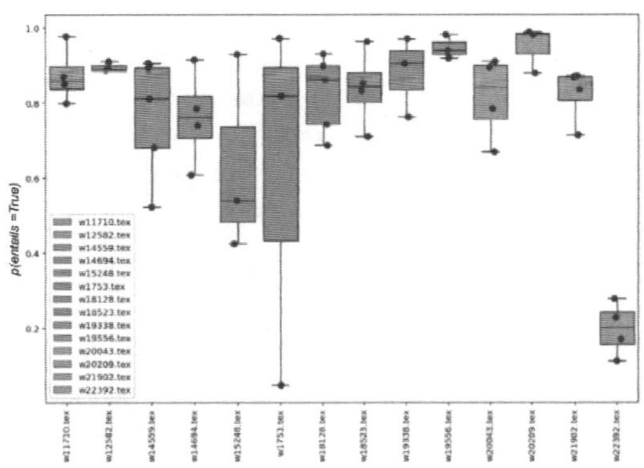

Figure 3: Distribution of scores for whether claims from the generated introductions *entail* the original introduction based on an LLM.

ligence. Two of the six spoke English as a second language and all participants spoke at least one language other than English.

The semi-structured interviews covered the following topics: participants' current approaches to find and validate references, if their approaches would change with unlimited time and resources, how their approach differs depending on citation type, and imagined capabilities of an ideal support tool for citation verification and recommendation. We performed inductive thematic analysis of the interviewees' statements. We performed three rounds of coding to create themes, resolving disagreements through conversation among two authors.

Time constraints limit the validation process. Nearly all participants raised the concern of careful validation. That is, they needed to understand specifically how the citation was relevant. However, several participants mentioned time constraints influencing their decision to cite works. Although every participant indicated that they sometimes cited papers that they had fully read, they also noted instances where they cited papers they had not entirely read. They employed skimming strategies while engaged in the literature review process in order to find more precisely related works.

Participants suggested various affordances for a tool to support the validation process. For example, one participant suggested finding the specific claims in the suggested citation that were related to the author's citing text. Going to the original source was important because some participants remarked that papers' claims can be misrepresented by citing authors, or the abstract did not accurately reflect the paper's results. In interfaces for scholarly readers, existing systems such as *Relatedly* (Palani et al., 2023) provide affordances similar to those suggested by the participants. The system we presented in this work only surfaces paper metadata such as title and abstract, so incorporating additional sensemaking affordances as part of the user's workflow will support more rigorous citation suggestion.

Surrounding text must be accurately scoped. Participants also stressed the importance of having nuanced enough statements to accurately represent the paper [P1,P2]. They recognized that inaccurate corresponding text is often the consequences of human error or time constraints, rather than bad faith actions. Therefore, P2 expressed interest in support for rewriting existing text spans to better represent the cited paper. Our work finds a reference from a text span. Future work could also improve an existing span to better represent the reference.

Community norms impact reference choices. Some participants felt pressure to cite "the right" source because peer reviewers would easily identify gaps in the related work. However, the precision of those citations varied depending on the field and relevance to the author's work. Several suggested that the situating citations might be more interchangeable than the more recent works.

Importance of contextualization within the broader literature. Participants reflected that although a given citation may be relevant, it may not be sufficient [P3,P4]. For instance, multiple references may be needed if the statement is multifaceted and nuanced, or if the statement is broad and requires a set of references. This idea of sufficiency extended to the reference set of entire sections, as P1 expressed concerns about misrepresenting sub-fields when merging or combining subsections of a related work.

Part of the challenge of building a good reference set is understanding the broader trends of the overall field. Participants expressed interest in a tool that bridges relevant but separate streams of the literature, whether it be similar methods and theories from a different field or differing methods and theories from a similar field [P1,P2,P3]. The challenge of becoming aware of and fully encapsulating these different strands motivated their wish for a tool with a broad sense of the literature. These reflections suggest that reference selection must be valid on multiple levels, with each individual reference accurately represented in the close text and the set of references sufficient in representing the overall literature. Our tool focuses on the former, and there is a rich opportunity for future work in the latter.

5 Conclusion

As a highly developed, precise form of communication, the skill set of academic writing takes time to develop. The writing process requires focus, yet can be disrupted by related tasks such as the curation of related work. The qualitative research showed that even experienced authors have nuanced procedures for identifying and citing prior work. Rather than fully replace academic authors, it seems more likely that writing assistants will continue to proliferate, capturing a rich design space (Lee et al., 2024). In this paper, we presented two affordances for academic writing framed in the context of a live authoring experience: suggesting citations in the context of the document, and writing an introduction section. Quantitative evaluation shows that these methods are capable of generating content that augments the author's writing process.

6 Limitations

The system, studies, and participants described herein were only evaluated on English-language documents and queries, although five of the six participants were fluent in a language other than English. The OpenAlex corpus includes non-English documents, but we excluded those from our database. Finally, citation suggestion is an inherently biased task. Simple filters such as citation count prevent the discovery of "sleeping beauties" (van Raan, 2004), while heuristics such as the venue's impact factor may obscure novel ideas that have not made it into mainstream publication. Systems that take diverse viewpoints into account, and present them to authors in an interpretable fashion, will help diffuse novel ideas into scientific discourse.

7 Acknowledgments

We thank Paul Raccuglia for work that inspired this project, Eun-Ah Kim for feedback on situating introduction sections of scholarly manuscripts, and John Platt for reviewing early generative output. We acknowledge the contribution of open-source contributors to Python packages including but not limited to `pylatexenc`, `TexSoup`, `bibtexparser`, and `more_itertools`.

References

Rohaid Ali, Oliver Y. Tang, Ian David Connolly, Patricia L. Zadnik Sullivan, J. H. Shin, Jared S. Fridley, Wael Asaad, Deus Cielo, Adetokunbo A. Oyelese, Curtis E. Doberstein, Ziya L. Gokaslan, and Albert E. Telfeian. 2023. Performance of ChatGPT and GPT-4 on neurosurgery written board examinations. *Neurosurgery*, 93:1353–1365.

Zafar Ali, Guilin Qi, Irfan Ullah, Adam A. Q. Mohammed, Pavlos Kefalas, and Khan Muhammad. 2024. GLAMOR: Graph-based LAnguage MOdel embedding for citation Recommendation. In *Proceedings of the 18th ACM Conference on Recommender Systems*, RecSys '24, page 929–933, New York, NY, USA. Association for Computing Machinery.

American Chemical Society. Professional Skills & Competencies - American Chemical Society — acs.org. `https://www.acs.org/education/policies/acs-approval-program/guidelines/professional-skills.html`. [Accessed 7 January 2025].

Iz Beltagy, Kyle Lo, and Arman Cohan. 2019. SciBERT: A pretrained language model for scientific text. In *Proceedings of the 2019 Conference on Empirical Methods in Natural Language Processing and the 9th International Joint Conference on Natural Language Processing (EMNLP-IJCNLP)*, pages 3615–3620, Hong Kong, China. Association for Computational Linguistics.

Jaroslav Borovička, Lars P Hansen, and José A Scheinkman. 2014. Misspecified recovery. Working Paper 20209, National Bureau of Economic Research.

Ralph Allan Bradley and Milton E. Terry. 1952. Rank analysis of incomplete block designs. *Biometrika*, 39:324–335.

Harry Bruce, William Jones, and Susan Dumais. 2004. Keeping and re-finding information on the web: What do people do and what do they need? *Proceedings of the American Society for Information Science and Technology*, 41(1):129–137.

Xi Chen, Paul N. Bennett, Kevyn Collins-Thompson, and Eric Horvitz. 2013. Pairwise ranking aggregation in a crowdsourced setting. In *Proceedings of the Sixth ACM International Conference on Web Search and Data Mining*, WSDM '13, page 193–202, New York, NY, USA. Association for Computing Machinery.

Florin Cuconasu, Giovanni Trappolini, Federico Siciliano, Simone Filice, Cesare Campagnano, Yoelle Maarek, Nicola Tonellotto, and Fabrizio Silvestri. 2024. The power of noise: Redefining retrieval for RAG systems. In *Proceedings of the 47th International ACM SIGIR Conference on Research and Development in Information Retrieval*, SIGIR '24, page 719–729, New York, NY, USA. Association for Computing Machinery.

Linda S. Flower and J. R. Hayes. 1981. A cognitive process theory of writing. *College Composition & Communication*.

John Flowerdew. 1999. Writing for scholarly publication in English: The case of Hong Kong. *Journal of Second Language Writing*, 8(2):123–145.

Michael Färber and Adam Jatowt. 2020. Citation recommendation: approaches and datasets. *International Journal on Digital Libraries*, 21(4):375–405.

Catherine A. Gao, Frederick M. Howard, Nikolay S. Markov, Emma C. Dyer, Siddhi Ramesh, Yuan Luo, and Alexander T. Pearson. 2023a. Comparing scientific abstracts generated by ChatGPT to real abstracts with detectors and blinded human reviewers. *npj Digital Medicine*, 6(1):75.

Yunfan Gao, Yun Xiong, Xinyu Gao, Kangxiang Jia, Jinliu Pan, Yuxi Bi, Yi Dai, Jiawei Sun, Qianyu Guo, Meng Wang, and Haofen Wang. 2023b. Retrieval-augmented generation for large language models: A survey. *ArXiv*, abs/2312.10997.

Katy Gero, Vivian Liu, and Lydia Chilton. 2022a. Sparks: Inspiration for science writing using language models. In *Proceedings of the First Workshop on Intelligent and Interactive Writing Assistants (In2Writing 2022)*, pages 83–84, Dublin, Ireland. Association for Computational Linguistics.

Katy Ilonka Gero, Vivian Liu, and Lydia Chilton. 2022b. Sparks: Inspiration for science writing using language models. In *Proceedings of the 2022 ACM Designing Interactive Systems Conference*, DIS '22, page 1002–1019, New York, NY, USA. Association for Computing Machinery.

Tom Hope, Doug Downey, Oren Etzioni, Daniel S. Weld, and Eric Horvitz. 2022. A computational inflection for scientific discovery. *Communications of the ACM*, 66:62–73.

Shamsi T. Iqbal, Jaime Teevan, Daniel J. Liebling, and Anne Loomis Thompson. 2018. Multitasking with Play Write, a mobile microproductivity writing tool. In *Proceedings of the 31st Annual ACM Symposium on User Interface Software and Technology*, UIST '18, page 411–422, New York, NY, USA. Association for Computing Machinery.

Ziwei Ji, Nayeon Lee, Rita Frieske, Tiezheng Yu, Dan Su, Yan Xu, Etsuko Ishii, Ye Jin Bang, Andrea Madotto, and Pascale Fung. 2023. Survey of hallucination in natural language generation. *ACM Computing Surveys*, 55(12).

Saurabh Kataria, Prasenjit Mitra, and Sumit Bhatia. 2010. Utilizing context in generative Bayesian models for linked corpus. *Proceedings of the AAAI Conference on Artificial Intelligence*, 24(1):1340–1345.

Mina Lee, Katy Ilonka Gero, John Joon Young Chung, Simon Buckingham Shum, Vipul Raheja, Hua Shen, Subhashini Venugopalan, Thiemo Wambsganss, David Zhou, Emad A. Alghamdi, Tal August, Avinash Bhat, Madiha Zahrah Choksi, Senjuti Dutta, Jin L.C. Guo, Md Naimul Hoque, Yewon Kim, Simon Knight, Seyed Parsa Neshaei, Antonette

Shibani, Disha Shrivastava, Lila Shroff, Agnia Sergeyuk, Jessi Stark, Sarah Sterman, Sitong Wang, Antoine Bosselut, Daniel Buschek, Joseph Chee Chang, Sherol Chen, Max Kreminski, Joonsuk Park, Roy Pea, Eugenia Ha Rim Rho, Zejiang Shen, and Pao Siangliulue. 2024. A design space for intelligent and interactive writing assistants. In *Proceedings of the 2024 CHI Conference on Human Factors in Computing Systems*, CHI '24, New York, NY, USA. Association for Computing Machinery.

Xiangci Li and Jessica Ouyang. 2024. Related work and citation text generation: A survey. In *Proceedings of the 2024 Conference on Empirical Methods in Natural Language Processing*, pages 13846–13864, Miami, Florida, USA. Association for Computational Linguistics.

Chin-Yew Lin. 2004. ROUGE: A package for automatic evaluation of summaries. In *Text Summarization Branches Out*, pages 74–81, Barcelona, Spain. Association for Computational Linguistics.

Kyle Lo, Lucy Lu Wang, Mark Neumann, Rodney Kinney, and Daniel Weld. 2020. S2ORC: The Semantic Scholar Open Research Corpus. In *Proceedings of the 58th Annual Meeting of the Association for Computational Linguistics*, pages 4969–4983. Association for Computational Linguistics.

Aman Madaan, Niket Tandon, Prakhar Gupta, Skyler Hallinan, Luyu Gao, Sarah Wiegreffe, Uri Alon, Nouha Dziri, Shrimai Prabhumoye, Yiming Yang, Shashank Gupta, Bodhisattwa Prasad Majumder, Katherine Hermann, Sean Welleck, Amir Yazdanbakhsh, and Peter Clark. 2023. Self-refine: Iterative refinement with self-feedback. In *Advances in Neural Information Processing Systems*, volume 36, pages 46534–46594. Curran Associates, Inc.

Cerstin Mahlow. 2023. Writing tools: Looking back to look ahead. *Preprint*, arXiv:2303.17894.

Meredith Ringel Morris. 2023. Scientists' perspectives on the potential for generative AI in their fields. *arXiv preprint arXiv:2304.01420*.

Emi Nakamura, Jósef Sigurdsson, and Jón Steinsson. 2016. The gift of moving: Intergenerational consequences of a mobility shock. Working Paper 22392, National Bureau of Economic Research.

Srishti Palani, Aakanksha Naik, Doug Downey, Amy X. Zhang, Jonathan Bragg, and Joseph Chee Chang. 2023. Relatedly: Scaffolding literature reviews with existing related work sections. In *Proceedings of the 2023 CHI Conference on Human Factors in Computing Systems*, CHI '23, New York, NY, USA. Association for Computing Machinery.

Jason Priem, Heather A. Piwowar, and Richard Orr. 2022. OpenAlex: A fully-open index of scholarly works, authors, venues, institutions, and concepts. *CoRR*, abs/2205.01833.

Zhen Qin, Rolf Jagerman, Kai Hui, Honglei Zhuang, Junru Wu, Le Yan, Jiaming Shen, Tianqi Liu, Jialu Liu, Donald Metzler, Xuanhui Wang, and Michael Bendersky. 2024. Large language models are effective text rankers with pairwise ranking prompting. In *Findings of the Association for Computational Linguistics: NAACL 2024*, pages 1504–1518, Mexico City, Mexico. Association for Computational Linguistics.

Yuval Reif and Roy Schwartz. 2024. Beyond performance: Quantifying and mitigating label bias in LLMs. In *Proceedings of the 2024 Conference of the North American Chapter of the Association for Computational Linguistics: Human Language Technologies (Volume 1: Long Papers)*, pages 6784–6798, Mexico City, Mexico. Association for Computational Linguistics.

Federico Ruggeri, Mohsen Mesgar, and Iryna Gurevych. 2023. A dataset of argumentative dialogues on scientific papers. In *Proceedings of the 61st Annual Meeting of the Association for Computational Linguistics (Volume 1: Long Papers)*, pages 7684–7699, Toronto, Canada. Association for Computational Linguistics.

Lin Shi, Chiyu Ma, Wenhua Liang, Weicheng Ma, and Soroush Vosoughi. 2024. Judging the judges: A systematic study of position bias in LLM-as-a-judge. *Preprint*, arXiv:2406.07791.

Amanpreet Singh, Mike D'Arcy, Arman Cohan, Doug Downey, and Sergey Feldman. 2023. SciRepEval: A multi-format benchmark for scientific document representations. In *Proceedings of the 2023 Conference on Empirical Methods in Natural Language Processing*, pages 5548–5566, Singapore. Association for Computational Linguistics.

Philip Sun, David Simcha, Dave Dopson, Ruiqi Guo, and Sanjiv Kumar. 2024. SOAR: improved indexing for approximate nearest neighbor search. In *Proceedings of the 37th International Conference on Neural Information Processing Systems*, NIPS '23, Red Hook, NY, USA. Curran Associates Inc.

Anthony F. J. van Raan. 2004. Sleeping Beauties in science. *Scientometrics*, 59(3):467–472.

Qingyun Wang, Lifu Huang, Zhiying Jiang, Kevin Knight, Heng Ji, Mohit Bansal, and Yi Luan. 2019. PaperRobot: Incremental draft generation of scientific ideas. In *Proceedings of the 57th Annual Meeting of the Association for Computational Linguistics*, pages 1980–1991, Florence, Italy. Association for Computational Linguistics.

Barbara M. Wildemuth and Ann L. O'Neill. 1995. The "known" in known-item searches: Empirical support for user-centered design (research note). *College & Research Libraries*, 56(3):265–281.

Ann Yuan, Andy Coenen, Emily Reif, and Daphne Ippolito. 2022. Wordcraft: Story writing with large language models. In *Proceedings of the 27th International Conference on Intelligent User Interfaces*, IUI '22, page 841–852, New York, NY, USA. Association for Computing Machinery.

Prompts templates are processed using the Jinja[3] templating library. Line breaks shown here may not match the line breaks used in the text prompt.

A Prompts for suggesting citations

A.1 Citation fabrication

```
You are an expert at suggesting relevant scientific papers.

I will provide some sentences from a paper that I am writing. In the sentences,
I will place a token CITE-HERE where I need to cite a relevant paper. Your task
is to make up the title and abstract of a paper that you think would be relevant
to this context. Give your output in JSON format with values for keys "title"
and "abstract".

SENTENCES: {{ previous_sentence }} {{ masked_sentence }} {{ next_sentence }}

Now, make up the title and abstract of a paper that I should cite at the CITE-HERE token.

Answer:
```

A.2 Citation scoring

```
You are the editor at a prestigious scientific journal. The author of a paper asks
you to recommend the best citation to support their claim. You are given a set of
citations of papers in JSON format. Each citation includes a key in the "key" field,
the paper title in the "title" field, and the paper abstract in the "abstract" field.
You are also given an extraction of the paper, which indicates the location of the
desired citation with the string "CITE-HERE".

Select the best citation from the list of citations that best supports the context
of the extraction and give the value of the corresponding "key" field. Only give me
the value, nothing else.

EXTRACTION
{{ previous_sentence }} {{ masked_sentence }}  {{ next_sentence }}

CITATIONS
[{% for c in citations %}
{
  'key': {{ c['key'] }},
  'title': {{ c['title'] }},
  'abstract': {{ c['abstract'] }},
}
{% endfor %}

The key of the citation that best fits this extraction is:
```

[3]https://jinja.palletsprojects.com/en/stable/

B Prompts for writing introductions

B.1 Determining claims

Extracts claims from the author's manuscript and compares them with existing work.

```
Your task is to determine if a paragraph from a scientific paper discusses
a novel result. You are given the abstract of the paper, abstract of related
paper, and a paragraph from the body of the paper. You answer YES if and only
if the paragraph's content is related to the abstract of this paper, and it
is novel relative to the abstracts of related papers.

ABSTRACT OF THIS PAPER
{{ abstract }}

ABSTRACT OF A RELATED PAPER
{{ ref_chunk[1].abstract }}

PARAGRAPH FROM THIS PAPER
{{ ref_chunk[0] }}

QUESTION
Q: Does the paragraph from this paper show a novel result worth mentioning
in the introduction? Respond YES or NO and explain your answer in one
sentence.
A:
```

B.2 Summarizing claims

Summarizes claims extracted using the previous prompt.

Inputs: `novel_results`, a list of text chunks from a paper.

```
You are a scientist writing up the results of your work. The following
paragraphs contain information about your results. Summarize the key
results in a few sentences.

{% for result in novel_results %}
  {{ result | trim }}
{% endfor %}

Now summarize the results in a few sentences.
```

B.3 Composing introduction

Final step in the prompt chain to compose the introduction section. Inputs:

Field name	Description
`title`	Manuscript title
`results`	Summary of experimental results
`[genesis_references]`	List of canonical references
`[recent_references]`	List of recent references

```
Given a list of related work, and the results of a paper, write the
introduction section for that paper. Refer to any of the REFERENCE
papers using the id in that REFERENCE.

PAPER TITLE: {{ title }}
```

```
FUNDAMENTAL PAPERS IN THIS FIELD:

{% for ref in genesis_references -%}
REFERENCE #{{ loop.index }}:
{% if ref.title is not none %}Title: "{{ ref.title }}"{% endif %}
{% if ref.abstract is not none %}Abstract: "{{ ref.abstract }}"{% endif %}
{% endfor -%}

RECENT RESULTS THAT THIS PAPER BUILDS ON:

{% for ref in recent_references -%}
REFERENCE #{{ loop.index + len(genesis_references) }}:
{% if ref.title is not none %}Title: "{{ ref.title }}"{% endif %}
{% if ref.abstract is not none %}Abstract: "{{ ref.abstract }}"{% endif %}
{% endfor -%}

RESULTS: {{ results }}

Now write the paper introduction. Cite references from both the FUNDAMENTAL PAPERS and
the RECENT RESULTS. When you cite a reference, use the reference number in brackets.
Begin and end your introduction with three single quotes (''').
{%- endsection -%}

INTRODUCTION:
```

B.4 Claim extraction (for evaluation)

Inputs: num_claims, the number of claims to extract from introduction, the text of the introduction.

```
Your job is to answer questions about the following introduction section of an
academic paper:

{{introduction}}

List {{num_claims}} novel claims that the introduction section makes. Output only
one sentence per claim and do not add additional explanation. Do not add any additional
formatting. Begin each claim with a number.
```

B.5 Entailment (for evaluation)

This prompt was used for evaluation.

```
You will be given a generated paragraph (hypothesis) and the text corresponding
to the original introduction (context). Your goal is to evaluate whether the
generated paragraph (hypothesis) entails the original introduction.

It is alright if the generated paragraph does not encompass the core of the
original introduction, as long as the generated paragraph does not introduce
any new claims.

Start your answer with "yes" or "no" depending on whether the generated
paragraph entails the original introduction and then provide a brief 1-2
sentence explanation for why.

GENERATED PARAGRAPH (hypothesis):
```

```
{{gen_intro_para}}

Original introduction (context):
{{orig_intro}}

Use the following format:
<yes or no depending on whether hypothesis entails the context>

Explanation:
```

C Generated output

*This **AI-generated text** is the system's output using the introduction writing method, applied to this manuscript. The system did not have access to the human-authored introduction at the time of generation.*

The proliferation of academic literature presents challenges for researchers seeking to efficiently locate and incorporate relevant prior work into their writing. Citation recommendation systems aim to alleviate this burden by suggesting relevant citations given a user's writing context. Early approaches to this task relied on representing academic works using topic models (Kataria et al., 2010) or embedding techniques (Beltagy et al., 2019), while graph-based methods leveraged citation networks to identify relevant work (Ali et al., 2024). While these methods can identify broadly relevant papers, they often fail to capture the nuanced ways in which researchers incorporate citations within their writing.

A key challenge in citation recommendation is the need for systems to understand not only the topical relevance of a citation, but also its specific role within the author's argument. Färber and Jatowt (2020) provide a comprehensive overview of pre-LLM techniques for citation recommendation, highlighting the limitations of existing methods in capturing this contextual information. More recent work has explored the use of large language models (LLMs) for citation recommendation, leveraging their ability to process and understand natural language (Gao et al., 2023b). These LLM-based approaches have shown promise in improving the accuracy and relevance of citation recommendations.

In this paper, we present a novel approach to AI-assisted academic writing that combines contextual citation recommendation with automated introduction generation. Our system leverages the power of LLMs to provide researchers with in-situ citation suggestions, recommending citations that are both topically relevant and appropriate for the specific context of their writing.

We demonstrate the effectiveness of our approach through a quantitative evaluation on a dataset of academic papers. Our results show that our system is able to accurately identify relevant citations, even when presented with limited context. Furthermore, we find that our system is able to generate coherent and informative introductions that accurately reflect the key contributions of a research paper.

Beyond simply identifying relevant citations, our system is designed to support the broader process of academic writing. Recognizing that researchers often struggle to synthesize and integrate prior work into their own writing, we incorporate a novel introduction generation component that automatically generates structured introductions, situating the contributions of a research paper within the context of prior work. This component leverages LLMs to identify the novel contributions of a paper, summarize related work, and compose a coherent introduction that effectively sets the stage for the research presented in the manuscript.

Evaluating and Enhancing Large Language Models for Novelty Assessment in Scholarly Publications

Ethan Lin *
Santa Clara University
Santa Clara, CA, USA
enlin@scu.edu

Zhiyuan Peng *
Santa Clara University
Santa Clara, CA, USA
zpeng@scu.edu

Yi Fang
Santa Clara University
Santa Clara, CA, USA
yfang@scu.edu

Abstract

Recent studies have evaluated creativity, where novelty is an important aspect, of large language models (LLMs) primarily from a semantic perspective, using benchmarks from cognitive science. However, assessing the novelty in scholarly publications, a critical facet of evaluating LLMs as scientific discovery assistants, remains underexplored, despite its potential to accelerate research cycles and prioritize high-impact contributions in scientific workflows. We introduce SchNovel [1], a benchmark to evaluate LLMs' ability to assess novelty in scholarly papers, a task central to streamlining the discovery pipeline. SchNovel consists of 15000 pairs of papers across six fields sampled from the arXiv dataset with publication dates spanning 2 to 10 years apart. In each pair, the more recently published paper is assumed to be more novel. Additionally, we propose RAG-Novelty, a retrieval-augmented method that mirrors human peer review by grounding novelty assessment in the retrieved context. Extensive experiments provide insights into the capabilities of different LLMs to assess novelty and demonstrate that RAG-Novelty outperforms recent baseline models, highlighting LLMs' promise as tools for automating novelty detection in scientific workflows.

1 Introduction

AI-driven scientific discovery systems, such as autonomous lab platforms like Coscientist (Boiko et al., 2023), promise to accelerate research by synthesizing insights from vast literature. A critical bottleneck, however, lies in identifying which papers introduce truly novel concepts, a capability essential for prioritizing experiments, avoiding redundant work, and guiding discovery pipelines. While large language models (LLMs) are increasingly deployed to analyze scientific texts, their ability to detect scholarly novelty, particularly in evolving research contexts, remains unproven. This gap persists despite LLMs' remarkable proficiency in tasks requiring creativity, traditionally defined as producing ideas that are both novel and effective (Runco and Jaeger, 2012). LLMs now solve open-domain problems, write code, and even generate research ideas rivaling human experts' novelty (Si et al., 2024). Yet their capacity to systematically assess novelty in scholarly publications, where contributions build incrementally on prior work, remains underexplored.

Recent studies evaluating the generative creativity of LLMs have yielded inconsistent conclusions. Orwig et al. (2024) concluded that GPT-4 (OpenAI, 2023) generates stories that are comparable to those written by humans in terms of creativity. Similarly, Pépin et al. (2024) found that LLMs can even surpass humans in specific creative tasks, such as divergent association and creative writing. However, Anderson et al. (2024) argued that AI-based creativity support tools (CSTs) like ChatGPT are not yet well-suited to fostering truly original ideas, as they can lead to the homogenization of human creativity. Chakrabarty et al. (2024) observed that LLM-generated stories pass the Torrance Test for Creative Writing (TTCW) tests 3 to 10 times less frequently than those written by professionals. Additionally, Chakrabarty et al. (2023) pointed out that LLMs often rely on cliches, produce text lacking nuance, and frequently resort to overly moralistic and predictable endings in stories. These discrepancies can be attributed to using different evaluation benchmarks and metrics, highlighting the lack of widely accepted standards for accessing LLM creativity in domain-specific contexts like scientific discovery.

The evaluation benchmarks used in current studies are primarily derived from cognitive science, such as the Torrance Tests of Creative Thinking (TTCT) (Lissitz and Willhoft, 1985), Alternative

*These authors contributed equally to this work.

[1]The SchNovel dataset and RAG-Novelty code are available at: https://github.com/ethannlin/SchNovel

Proceedings of the 1st Workshop on AI and Scientific Discovery: Directions and Opportunities, pages 46–57
May 3, 2025

Use Task (AUT) (Guilford, 1964), and the Runco Creativity Assessment Battery (rCAB) (Runco, 2011). These benchmarks focus on assessing semantic creativity by tasks like generating responses to pictures or listing as many uses as possible for a common object. Corresponding metrics include fluency, flexibility, originality, and elaboration. However, these metrics primarily assess semantic novelty, which does not fully capture the kind of novelty emphasized in scholarly research. Novelty in scholarly work is especially critical, as each paper undergoes rigorous peer review, particularly in high-prestige venues. Novel papers typically build upon existing research while introducing new ideas, methods, or insights, making novelty assessment heavily dependent on current and past trends in research.

While LLMs have shown great capability in generating text and mimicking human reasoning, their ability to assess novelty in scholarly publications remains largely unexamined. To address this gap, we present a scholarly novelty benchmark (SchNovel) to evaluate LLMs' capability of assessing novelty in scholarly papers. Specifically, we leverage the arXiv dataset to create a collection of 15,000 paper pairs. In each pair, we assume that the more recently published paper is more novel. Papers are selected across six categories, with publication dates spaced by gaps ranging from 2 to 10 years between the paired papers. We evaluate various LLMs on their ability to assess novelty and report their accuracy.

To further improve novelty assessment, we propose RAG-Novelty, a retrieval-augmented generation method. This method assumes that more novel papers will retrieve more recently published works, enhancing the novelty prediction. Our extensive experiments demonstrate that RAG-Novelty outperforms recent baseline models in assessing novelty in scholarly papers. Our key contributions include:

- We release the first benchmark, SchNovel, specifically designed to evaluate LLMs' capability in assessing novelty within scholarly publications.
- We conduct comprehensive experiments to explore how variations in categories, starting years, and year gaps affect LLMs' ability to assess paper novelty.
- We propose a novel method, RAG-Novelty, to enhance LLMs' performance in assessing paper novelty.

2 Related Work

2.1 Existing Benchmarks

TTCT (Lissitz and Willhoft, 1985) is a commercially protected assessment tool consisting of six tasks: 1) asking a question about a picture; 2) guessing the cause of the action depicted in the image; 3) predicting the consequences of the action described in the image; 4) improving a product described in 2-3 sentences in the most interesting and unusual way; 5) suggesting interesting and unconventional uses for a given item; and 6) imagining what would happen if an improbable situation were to occur. Both AUT (Guilford, 1964) and rCAB (Runco, 2011) ask participants to generate as many uses as possible for a common object. The Remote Associates Test (RAT) (Mednick and Halpern, 1968) presents participants with three seemingly unrelated words and asks them to find a fourth word that connects all three. The Consensual Assessment Technique (CAT) (Amabile, 1982) evaluates creative products, such as stories, poetry, dramatic performances, and musical compositions, using a panel of domain experts. The Wallach-Kogan Creativity Tests (WCT) (Brody, 1966) consist of the AUT, Instances Test, and Similarities Test. The Scholarly Creativity Test (SCT) (Hu and Adey, 2002) measures scholarly creativity and process skills. The Divergent Association Task (DAT) (Olson et al., 2021) asks participants to name unrelated nouns and calculates the pairwise semantic distance between them. However, all these existing cognitive science benchmarks are not suited for evaluating LLMs' capability to assess novelty in scholarly publications, a gap our proposed benchmark addresses.

2.2 Creativity and Novelty Assessment

Traditional general novelty assessment methods use pre-defined metrics like the similarity to existing methods (Just et al., 2024) and the diversity of references (Shibayama et al., 2021) to score the novelty of a method or scholarly paper. To assess LLMs' capability of generating or assessing creativity and novelty, current studies employ different prompt strategies to interact with LLMs and collect responses for evaluation. Guzik et al. (2023) utilized a basic prompt to evaluate GPT-4 on the TTCT benchmark. Mehrotra et al. (2024) applied associative thinking (Mednick, 1962) in prompts designed for specific tasks like product design and marketing. Zhao et al. (2024) analyzed LLMs' responses to an expanded TTCT benchmark, applying diverse prompts, including basic prompts, instructive prompts, post-instructive prompts, and Chain of Thought (CoT) prompts. Stevenson et al. (2022) demonstrates that defining the role of LLMs as "scientist" can improve performance. Summers-Stay et al. (2023) improves the basic prompt method used in (Stevenson et al., 2022) by using multi-step reasoning to enhance GPT-3's performance on AUT. Similar to the multi-round interaction framework utilized in LLM Debate (Du et al., 2024), LLM Discussion (Lu et al., 2024) develops a role-play-enhanced LLM discussion framework to augment ChatGPT's performance on the WCT and SCT benchmarks. Unlike existing prompting methods, our proposed RAG-Novelty improves the LLM's performance by retrieving similar papers, assuming that novel papers should retrieve the latest publications.

2.3 LLM Performance Evaluation

Most existing studies (Summers-Stay et al., 2023; Stevenson et al., 2022; Guzik et al., 2023; Mednick, 1962) evaluate LLM performance on benchmarks (Section 2.1) using human assessments. For example, Guzik et al. (2023) evaluated LLM responses to the TTCT, which were scored by Scholastic Testing Services (STS). Other studies rely on LLMs to score responses from another LLM. Zhao et al. (2024) used a more powerful GPT-4 to evaluate the performance of smaller LLMs, while Lu et al. (2024) utilized ChatGPT to assess responses generated by GPT-4. Additionally, Lu et al. (2024) compared LLM-generated scores with human evaluations, finding that LLM evaluations correlated more closely with the average human score. Both Luchini et al. (2023) and (Organisciak et al., 2023) fine-tuned models on human-scored data to evaluate LLM responses. Since our benchmark provides ground-truth binary labels, evaluation is straightforward.

3 Scholarly Novelty Benchmark

Unlike the semantic novelty evaluated by the benchmarks from cognitive science (Section 2.1), novelty in scholarly publications refers to introducing new ideas, methods, or discoveries that have previously not been explored or established in the literature. Evaluating novelty is fundamentally an exercise in understanding the relationship between ideas across time rather than simply assessing new ideas or techniques. This understanding is crucial in determining the contribution of a research paper. The assumption can be made that later works are more novel than prior works, as they typically introduce new ideas and methodologies in the current research climate (Beaty and Silvia, 2012; Acar et al., 2019). In this paper, we apply this assumption to establish ground truth values for our created benchmark SchNovel.

3.1 Dataset Collection and Structure

The arXiv dataset[2] comprises approximately 2.5 million articles, with the earliest dating back to 1986. All articles are categorized into eight distinct fields[3], each of which has some sub-fields. We picked six out of eight fields: Computer Science (cs), Mathematics (math), Physics (physics), Quantitative Biology (q-bio), Quantitative Finance (q-fin), and Statistics (stat), as we did not collect enough papers in other fields. Figure 6 in Appendix A.1 shows the number of papers published each year for each field. To assess the ability of LLMs to assess the novelty of research papers, we sampled a subset of articles from each field, denoted as dataset $D = \{(f, g, s, x, y, label)_i\}_{i=1}^{N}$ where $N = 15000$, following the procedure outlined in Algorithm 1 in Appendix A.4, where f represent the field, x and y represent the paper ids, s represents the year in which paper x was published, g represents the number of years paper y was published before paper x and $label$ equals to paper x as we assume in the same field, later published paper is more novel.

3.2 Tasks and Evaluation Metrics

We define the task as assessing which paper is more novel when given a pair of papers. Specifically, for each tuple $(f, g, s, x, y, label)_i$, the selected LLM is provided with the title, abstract, and optional metadata for each paper—information typically available to a reviewer. However, unlike a full review, the model does not have access to the full text, making the task more challenging. While the abstract offers a strong indication of a paper's content and key findings, important details may be missed. By limiting the context to the abstract and

[2]Available at https://www.kaggle.com/datasets/Cornell-University/arxiv

[3]See the full taxonomy at https://arxiv.org/category_taxonomy

metadata, we also improve efficiency in terms of token consumption and cost. We will discuss the potential limitations of this approach in Section 8. Various comparison methods, such as point-wise and pair-wise, can be employed, and we evaluate performance based on accuracy.

4 RAG-Novelty

Assessing the novelty in scholarly papers requires the model to have a good understanding of past and present works to accurately judge whether a paper is novel in the current research climate. However, once trained, LLMs are frozen in time, meaning that they are no longer updated with the latest information, so they lack this understanding of the field's current state. Inspired by RAG, we propose a novel method, RAG-Novelty, to further improve LLMs' capability to assess novelty in our benchmark. As shown in Figure 1, apart from the information, like abstract, that can be utilized for a paper, we apply the paper abstract as a query to retrieve top-K papers from the already built index, and then create a prompt based on the query paper and the retrieved papers to ask the LLM to score the novelty of the query paper from 0 to 10.

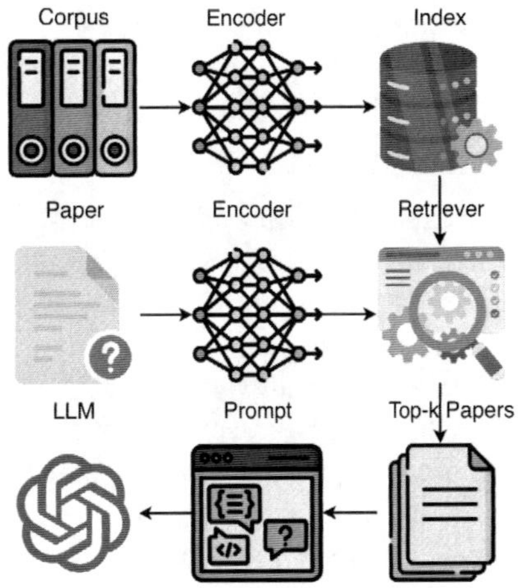

Figure 1: The overview of RAG-Novelty

4.1 Indexing and Retriever

To assess the novelty of a paper with the information provided by our SchNovel, such as title, abstract, and other metadata excluding the whole paper, an expert human reviewer in the same field may accurately score the novelty, a junior human reviewer, however, is likely not confident of scoring the novelty directly and instead will first review some similar papers and then assess the novelty. To mimic the review process taken by a human reviewer, we randomly sampled 500 papers from all years from 2000 to 2023, yielding 12000 papers for each field. Then, the abstracts of these papers are encoded into embeddings using OpenAI's *text-embedding-3-small*[4] model. The retrieval is the exact search method based on cosine similarity, as the number of candidates is very small. Our method can also handle huge candidate corpus by building an approximate nearest neighbor searching index using faiss (Douze et al., 2024; Johnson et al., 2019).

When a human reviewer conducts a literature search, it is naturally impossible to retrieve papers published after the query paper's publication date. To simulate this realistic constraint in our evaluation, we filtered out any papers published after the query paper and retrieved the top-k relevant papers from those published prior to or on the same date. However, in the context of pairwise comparisons, where we are assessing the novelty between two papers with different publication dates, it is reasonable to retrieve papers up to the publication date of the more recent paper. To prevent any leakage, we ensured that the papers themselves were excluded from the top-k retrieved documents. This approach mirrors a realistic scenario in which novelty is judged relative to the latest available knowledge at the time of publication. By implementing this strategy, we ensure that the novelty assessment remains fair and contextually appropriate, avoiding any temporal bias while maintaining the integrity of the comparison.

4.2 Prompt

We first compared the zero-shot, two-shot, and self-reflection prompts and found that the self-reflection prompt performed the best (Section 6.1). So, for RAG-Novelty, we built the prompt, shown in Appendix A.6, based on the self-reflection prompt, shown in Appendix A.3, by incorporating the information of the retrieved papers. Specifically, we added a "Contextual Data Analysis" instruction that assumes that the more recent papers are retrieved, the more novel this query paper is:

Average the published dates of the retrieved documents. Use this average date as additional context for your evaluation.

[4] https://platform.openai.com/docs/guides/embeddings

Consider that papers with an average date that is later or more recent in time are generally more novel.

5 Experimental Setup

5.1 Baseline Methods

Zero-Shot as shown in Appendix A.2, involves providing the model with two research papers' titles, abstracts, and four-step instructions, guiding the LLM to leverage its internal knowledge to make an informed decision. We also conducted a pointwise comparison by revising the zero-shot prompt to instruct the LLM score on the novelty of each paper first and then compare which one is more novel.

Two-Shot We randomly sampled two example paper pairs and added them to the zero-shot prompt.

Chain of Thought (CoT) (Wei et al., 2023) elicits reasoning within models by giving the model time to "think". We achieved CoT by adding instructions to Zero-Shot guiding LLMs to provide demonstrations.

Self-Reflection (Renze and Guven, 2024) has shown several strides in improving LLMs' logical fallacies by prompting the model to reflect on its incorrect solutions. We adopted this strategy to design a prompt, which is shown in Appendix A.3.

Self-Consistency (Wang et al., 2023) assumes that ground truth answers can be achieved through different reasoning paths. We followed the original paper to sample 10 generated sequences and voted majority.

LLM Discussion (Lu et al., 2024) assigns LLMs with different roles and lets them discuss with each other before making the final decision. We adopted LLM Discussion to simulate the review process taken by human reviewers. Specifically, we assume the papers are submitted to a conference to be reviewed, and we designed four roles: (a) a professor; (b) a PhD student; (c) an editor of a prestigious journal; (d) the chair of the conference where the professor, PhD student, and editor are all reviewers and they have two round discussions and the chair make the final decision. The prompt is shown in Appendix A.5.

5.2 LLM Configuration

We adopted the default settings of API [5] for Zero-Shot, Two-Shot, CoT, and RAG-Novelty. We followed the Self-Consistency to adopt the temperature as 0.7 and set the number of reasoning paths as 10. For LLM discussion, we limit the max tokens to 200 to avoid overwhelming the model with long inputs in subsequent rounds of discussion. For Self-consistency, we limit the max tokens so that the response is concise, as long reasoning for this task is unnecessary because we're looking for consistency rather than depth. In both cases, we prompt the model to limit its output to 150 tokens to ensure that its response fits within the 200 token limit.

[5] https://platform.openai.com/docs/guides/chat-completions

Method	cs	math	physics	qbio	qfin	stat
Zero-Shot	0.64	0.55	0.57	0.54	0.55	0.63
Two-Shot	0.62	0.55	0.57	0.54	0.55	0.60
CoT	0.63	0.56	0.57	0.54	0.56	0.62
Self-Reflection	0.65	0.56	0.58	0.56	0.57	0.63
LLM Discussion	0.60	0.55	0.56	0.53	0.50	0.58
Self-Consistency	<u>0.66</u>	<u>0.57</u>	<u>0.59</u>	<u>0.58</u>	<u>0.60</u>	<u>0.64</u>
RAG-Novelty	†0.72*	0.58*	†0.62*	†0.65*	†0.73*	†0.68*

Table 1: RAG-Novelty vs. Baselines on SchNovel with GPT-4o-mini. Averaged accuracy is reported. † denotes statistically significant enhancements over the second-best result, with p-values < 0.05, as determined by the McNemar test. The best results across different methods are denoted with the symbol ⋆. The second-best results across different methods are underlined.

5.3 Research Questions

This study aims to address several key questions regarding the performance of LLMs on the SchNovel benchmark.

- **R1:** Which comparison approach yields better results: pointwise or pairwise?
- **R2:** How do different LLMs perform in assessing the novelty of research papers?
- **R3** How does the category of the research paper affect the performance of LLMs?
- **R4:** How does the publication start year influence the performance of LLMs?
- **R5:** What impact does the gap between the publication years of research papers have on LLMs' performance?
- **R6:** What are the effects of other metadata attributes on LLMs' performance?
- **R7:** Can RAG-Novelty outperform recent baselines?

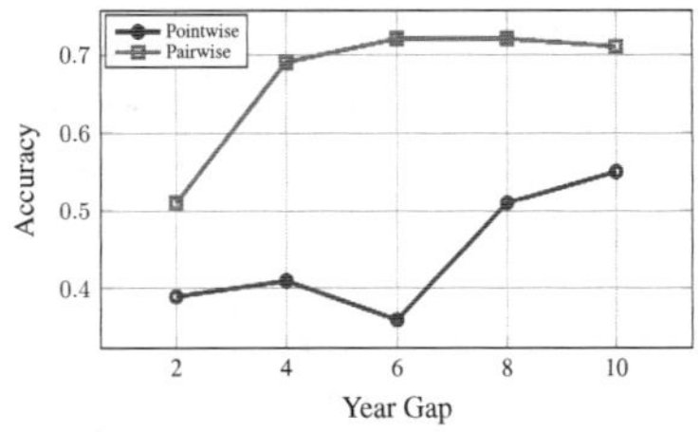

Figure 2: Pointwise vs. pairwise. The metrics above were obtained in the cs field with the start year $s = 2023$ and GPT-4o-mini.

6 Experimental Results

6.1 RAG-Novelty vs. Baseline Models (R7)

In this experiment, we evaluate the performance of RAG-Novelty against baseline methods. All methods use GPT-4o-mini, and the accuracy is averaged across different start years s and year gaps g. Pairwise comparison is applied to all methods, and we account for position bias by swapping the order of the two papers in the comparisons.

Two-Shot does not improve upon Zero-Shot as it typically does in other tasks. We attribute this to the complexity of the novelty assessment task, which requires deeper contextual understanding and comparison between papers—something that randomly selected examples may not effectively convey. Through iterative prompt refinement, Self-Reflection outperforms CoT in all fields except mathematics. LLM Discussion methods perform the worst, failing to even surpass Zero-Shot. Self-Consistency achieves the best results among baseline methods, demonstrating that obtaining answers through different reasoning paths helps improve performance. Our RAG-Novelty achieves the highest results overall, significantly outperforming the second-best method, except in the mathematics field. Across all methods, the improvement in mathematics is limited, possibly due to the slower progression of the field, the prevalence of symbols that LLMs struggle to interpret, or a lack of sufficient mathematical content in the training data compared to other fields.

6.2 Pointwise vs Pairwise (R1)

As mentioned in Section 5.1, we revised the pairwise Zero-Shot prompt (Appendix A.2) to a pointwise one. We compared the two methods by evaluating them in the cs field with the start year 2023, crossing different year gaps. As shown in Figure 2, pairwise is consistently much better than pointwise across different year gaps. This significant difference highlights the importance of context. As with human evaluations, providing relevant context or reference points is crucial for accurate assessments (Yan et al., 2022), allowing reviewers to consider the broad implications of a paper within the current research landscape. Pairwise comparisons align with this process, simplifying the task of considering the relative merits of two papers side-by-side rather than evaluating each one in isolation. Thus, pairwise comparisons are used in the rest of the following experiments.

6.3 The Impact of Different Fields (R3)

In Figure 3, the cs category shows the highest accuracy across most year gaps (starting in 2023), likely due to the availability of data and well-defined evaluation metrics. In contrast, math and physics show lower accuracy, likely due to domain-specific challenges such as complex notation in mathematics and theoretical frameworks in physics.

One explanation is the lack of domain knowledge in ChatGPT's training data, which, being sourced from the internet, may not adequately cover specialized fields. Research has shown that LLMs exhibit biases in various prompts and tasks (Cheng et al., 2023; Stranisci et al., 2023), suggesting potential categorical biases in lesser-known or slower-growing domains. This has significant implications for using AI tools in academia and industry, particularly in automated scoring or ranking systems, where such biases could perpetuate inequalities.

6.4 The Impact of Different Start Years and Year Gaps (R4 & R5)

To better understand how different start years affect the performance of LLMs in evaluating novelty, we investigated the model's results for five distinct start years. As shown in Figure 4, the model's results for all five start years were relatively consistent across different year gaps. This suggests that the model's ability to evaluate novelty between two papers is more dependent on the year gap between them than the specific publication years.

For example, evaluating two papers with a 10-year gap from 2009 to 2019 should be equivalent in difficulty to evaluating two papers with a 10-year gap from 2013 to 2023. Regardless of the boundary years within those ranges (i.e., considering papers published at specific points like 2009 and 2019, versus 2013 and 2023), it's the decade-long gap between the papers' publication times that makes

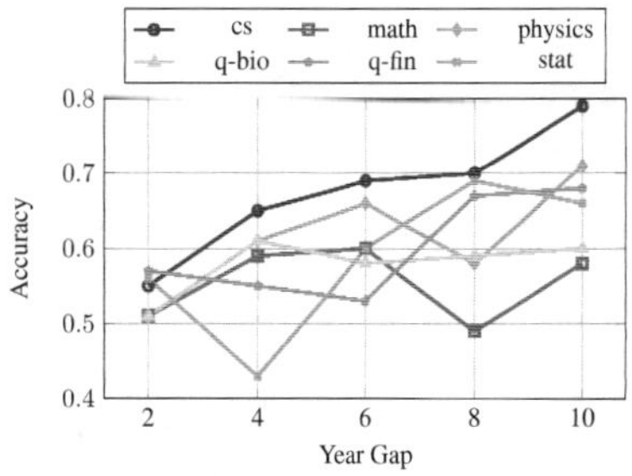

Figure 3: Comparison of fields. The metrics above were obtained using Self-Reflection in cs field with the start year $s = 2023$ with GPT-4o-mini.

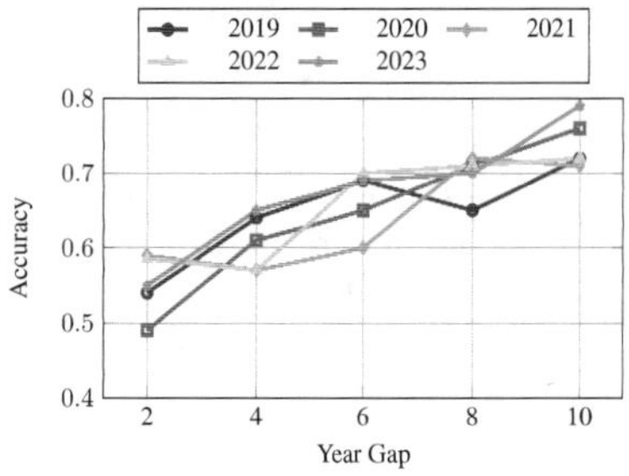

Figure 4: Comparison of Start Years. The metrics above were obtained using Self-Reflection in the cs field with GPT-4o-mini.

it easier for the model to make such a binary evaluation.

6.5 The Impact of Different LLMs (R2)

All LLMs can vary significantly depending on their training data and model architecture. With various different models available, it is essential to understand how they perform when assessing the originality of ideas presented in research papers. In this section, we examine the impact of using different LLMs on evaluating novelty.

Our findings in Table 2 reveal significant disparities in performance across different LLMs. GPT-4o-mini, GPT-3.5, and Gemma 2 performed more in line with expectations, achieving a more balanced distribution of predictions throughout all year gaps. Notably, GPT-4o-mini outperformed all other models, demonstrating a substantial advantage over smaller models like LLaMA 3.1-8b, Mistral 7b, and Gemma 2-9b.

Despite such success, even ChatGPT 4o-mini and ChatGPT 3.5 exhibit position bias, where the order of papers in the prompt affects their decision-making instead of content alone. This bias is magnified in smaller models, which lack extensive training compared to larger models. For example, Mistral 7b is heavily biased toward the last paper in the prompt. This aligns with known issues regarding LLMs' performance being best when relevant information appears towards the beginning or end of the prompt (Liu et al., 2024; Dai et al., 2024).

In contrast, LLaMA 3.1-8b exhibits a different bias, favoring the first paper that appears toward the middle of the prompt. According to Dubey et al. (2024), the LLaMA 3.1 models excel at "needle-in-the-haystack" tasks, where one needs to find specific information in large amounts of text (Kamradt, 2023), ultimately fixing the issues described in Liu et al. (2024). This is similar to skimming, which is efficient for finding specific information but may not facilitate deep understanding. Thus, while LLaMA 3.1-8b excels at retrieving specific information from anywhere in a context, this skillset is not ideal for evaluating novelty between two papers.

6.6 The Impact of Metadata (R6)

Previously, our experiments evaluated novelty based solely on a paper's title and abstract. However, human evaluations often take into account various metadata that can subtly influence reviewers' decisions. This metadata-induced bias has significant implications for research evaluations and highlights the need for more anonymous reviewal processes, leading to solutions such as double-blind reviewal processes. A pairwise comparison was applied for all the experiments in this section, and we accounted for position bias by swapping the order of the two papers in the comparisons.

6.6.1 Adding a TLDR Summary

We utilized the SciTLDR model (Cachola et al., 2020) from the Semantic Scholar API (Kinney et al., 2023) to generate TLDRs for our dataset, expecting this additional information to enhance accuracy by helping the model generalize and better understand the paper. As shown in Table 3, adding TLDRs decreases the accuracy across all year gaps. Nevertheless, incorporating such data did mitigate position bias, as evidenced by the negligible difference between ascending and descending year accuracies across nearly all year gaps.

6.6.2 Adding Author

We then added the author to the prompt, expecting that this additional information would not affect the model performance as the authors should not influence the novelty assessment. To our surprise, adding such information did help mitigate some

Year Gap	ChatGPT4o-mini			ChatGPT3.5			LLaMA 3.1-8b			Mistral-7b			Gemma-2-9b		
	Asc Yr	Desc Yr	Acc.	Asc Yr	Desc Yr	Acc.	Asc Yr	Desc Yr	Acc.	Asc Yr	Desc Yr	Acc.	Asc Yr	Desc Yr	Acc.
2	0.44	0.66	0.55	0.46	0.62	0.54	0.03	0.98	0.51	1.00	0.00	0.50	0.66	0.38	0.52
4	0.58	0.72	0.65	0.58	0.57	0.58	0.02	0.97	0.50	1.00	0.00	0.50	0.70	0.48	0.59
6	0.63	0.75	0.69	0.67	0.60	0.64	0.01	0.99	0.50	1.00	0.01	0.51	0.69	0.41	0.55
8	0.63	0.77	0.70	0.63	0.68	0.66	0.01	0.99	0.50	0.99	0.00	0.50	0.76	0.46	0.61
10	0.79	0.78	0.79	0.67	0.71	0.69	0.05	0.97	0.51	0.99	0.01	0.50	0.80	0.43	0.62
Average	0.61	0.74	0.68	0.60	0.64	0.62	0.02	0.98	0.50	0.996	0.004	0.50	0.72	0.43	0.58

Table 2: Comparison of different LLMs. The metrics above were obtained using Self-Reflection in the cs field with the start year $s = 2023$. "Asc Yr" indicates that the older paper is presented first in the prompt, while "Desc Yr" means the newer paper is presented first.

Year Gap	Zero-Shot			Self-Reflection			Self-Reflection w/ tldr			Self-Reflection 2 w/ author		
	Asc Yr	Desc Yr	Acc.	Asc Yr	Desc Yr	Acc.	Asc Yr	Desc Yr	Acc.	Asc Yr	Desc Yr	Acc.
2	0.41	0.60	0.51	0.44	0.66	0.55	**0.53**	**0.51**	0.52	**0.57**	**0.55**	0.56
4	0.63	0.74	0.69	0.58	0.72	0.65	**0.64**	**0.64**	0.64	0.67	0.62	0.65
6	0.64	0.79	0.72	0.63	0.75	0.69	**0.66**	**0.69**	0.68	0.75	0.62	0.69
8	0.66	0.77	0.72	0.63	0.77	0.70	0.69	0.61	0.65	**0.68**	**0.67**	0.68
10	0.64	0.78	0.71	0.78	0.79	0.79	**0.76**	**0.76**	0.76	0.80	0.75	0.78
Average	0.60	0.74	0.67	0.61	0.74	0.68	0.66	0.64	0.65	0.69	0.64	0.67

Table 3: The impact of metadata. The metrics above were obtained using Self-Reflection in the cs field with the start year $s = 2023$ and GPT-4o-mini. "Asc Yr" indicates that the older paper is presented first in the prompt, while "Desc Yr" means the newer paper is presented first.

of the position bias, as seen in the bold results in Table 3, but overall, it decreased the performance slightly.

6.6.3 Adding Affiliation

We selected two universities, one of which is a top research university and the other a teaching university, to study whether affiliation bias exists in LLMs' assessment of novelty.[6] Specifically, we first assigned the top research university as the affiliation of the more recently published paper and the teaching university to the earlier published paper, with the results shown in blue. Then, we swapped the affiliations, and the results are shown in red. As illustrated in Figure 5, the top research university starts with similar accuracy to the teaching university at a year gap of $g = 2$, but as the year gap increases, the top research university consistently outperforms the teaching university. This suggests that affiliation bias exists in LLMs' novelty assessments, with a tendency to "trust" papers from top research universities. However, although we observed LLMs' preference for choosing the top research university, the top research university experiments are undertaken without affiliation. This unexpected result raises questions about how LLMs process affiliation information, which warrants further investigation to better understand and mitigate such biases.

[6]The real names of the universities are not used to ensure objectivity and to avoid any unintended bias or implications.

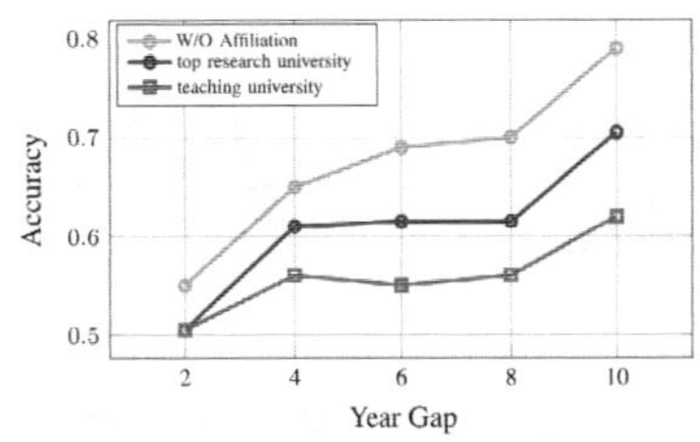

Figure 5: Comparison of different organizations. The metrics above were obtained using Self-Reflection in the cs field with start year $s = 2023$ and GPT-4o-mini.

7 Conclusion and Future Work

To evaluate LLMs' ability to assess novelty in scholarly publications, we introduce SchNovel, a benchmark consisting of 15,000 pairs of papers across six fields. We conducted extensive experiments to understand how various factors influence LLM performance on SchNovel. To enhance LLMs' capability to assess novelty, we propose RAG-Novelty, which significantly outperforms strong baseline models in comprehensive experiments. For future work, we plan to expand SchNovel by including more papers and covering additional fields to evaluate LLMs on a larger scale. Another promising direction is investigating which part of a paper best represents the whole for novelty assessment by LLMs. Additionally, studying how LLMs process affiliation and addressing biases in novelty evaluation, such as position and affiliation bias, is an important area for further research.

8 Limitations

Our study evaluates an LLM's ability to assess novelty using a research paper's title, abstract, and metadata. While the abstract provides a strong indication of a paper's content and key findings, it may not fully capture the novelty of the research compared to the complete text. Abstracts often summarize the main ideas but may omit important technical details. Although this approach streamlines the evaluation process, it could occasionally limit the depth of the novelty assessment due to the absence of a more comprehensive context.

Additionally, the exclusive use of arXiv data is limiting. We selected arXiv as an initial step for its broad, publicly accessible range of publications. Future work can improve robustness using peer-reviewed publications and sampling papers from more sources.

References

Selcuk Acar, Ahmed M. Abdulla Alabbasi, Mark A. Runco, and Kenes Beketayev. 2019. Latency as a predictor of originality in divergent thinking. *Think ing Skills and Creativity*.

Teresa M Amabile. 1982. Social psychology of creativity: A consensual assessment technique. *Journal of personality and social psychology*, 43(5):997.

Barrett R. Anderson, Jash Hemant Shah, and Max Kreminski. 2024. Homogenization effects of large language models on human creative ideation. In *Proceedings of the 16th Conference on Creativity & Cognition, Chicago, IL, USA, June 23-26, 2024*, pages 413–425. ACM.

Roger E. Beaty and Paul Silvia. 2012. Why do ideas get more creative across time? an executive interpretation of the serial order effect in divergent thinking tasks. *Psychology of Aesthetics, Creativity, and the Arts*, 6:309–319.

Daniil A Boiko, Robert MacKnight, Ben Kline, and Gabe Gomes. 2023. Autonomous chemical research with large language models. *Nature*, 624(7992):570–578.

Viola A Brody. 1966. Modes of thinking in young children: A study of the creativity-intelligence distinction. *Archives of General Psychiatry*, 14(3):329–331.

Isabel Cachola, Kyle Lo, Arman Cohan, and Daniel S. Weld. 2020. Tldr: Extreme summarization of scientific documents. *Preprint*, arXiv:2004.15011.

Tuhin Chakrabarty, Philippe Laban, Divyansh Agarwal, Smaranda Muresan, and Chien-Sheng Wu. 2024. Art or artifice? large language models and the false promise of creativity. In *Proceedings of the CHI Conference on Human Factors in Computing Systems, CHI 2024, Honolulu, HI, USA, May 11-16, 2024*, pages 30:1–30:34. ACM.

Tuhin Chakrabarty, Vishakh Padmakumar, Faeze Brahman, and Smaranda Muresan. 2023. Creativity support in the age of large language models: An empirical study involving emerging writers. *CoRR*, abs/2309.12570.

Myra Cheng, Esin Durmus, and Dan Jurafsky. 2023. Marked personas: Using natural language prompts to measure stereotypes in language models. In *Proceedings of the 61st Annual Meeting of the Association for Computational Linguistics (Volume 1: Long Papers)*, pages 1504–1532, Toronto, Canada. Association for Computational Linguistics.

Sunhao Dai, Chen Xu, Shicheng Xu, Liang Pang, Zhenhua Dong, and Jun Xu. 2024. Bias and unfairness in information retrieval systems: New challenges in the llm era. In *Proceedings of the 30th ACM SIGKDD Conference on Knowledge Discovery and Data Mining*, KDD '24, page 6437–6447, New York, NY, USA. Association for Computing Machinery.

Matthijs Douze, Alexandr Guzhva, Chengqi Deng, Jeff Johnson, Gergely Szilvasy, Pierre-Emmanuel Mazaré, Maria Lomeli, Lucas Hosseini, and Hervé Jégou. 2024. The faiss library.

Yilun Du, Shuang Li, Antonio Torralba, Joshua B. Tenenbaum, and Igor Mordatch. 2024. Improving factuality and reasoning in language models through multiagent debate. In *Forty-first International Conference on Machine Learning, ICML 2024, Vienna, Austria, July 21-27, 2024*. OpenReview.net.

Abhimanyu Dubey, Abhinav Jauhri, Abhinav Pandey, and et al. 2024. The llama 3 herd of models. *Preprint*, arXiv:2407.21783.

J Pv Guilford. 1964. Some new looks at the nature of creative processes. *Contributions to mathematical psychology. New York: Holt, Rinehart & Winston*.

Erik E Guzik, Christian Byrge, and Christian Gilde. 2023. The originality of machines: Ai takes the torrance test. *Journal of Creativity*, 33(3):100065.

Weiping Hu and Philip Adey. 2002. A scientific creativity test for secondary school students. *International Journal of Science Education*, 24(4):389–403.

Jeff Johnson, Matthijs Douze, and Hervé Jégou. 2019. Billion-scale similarity search with GPUs. *IEEE Transactions on Big Data*, 7(3):535–547.

Julian Just, Thomas Ströhle, Johann Füller, and Katja Hutter. 2024. Ai-based novelty detection in crowdsourced idea spaces. *Innovation*, 26(3):359–386.

Gregory Kamradt. 2023. Llmtest_needleinahaystack. `https://github.com/gkamradt/LLMTest_NeedleInAHaystack/blob/main/README.md`. Accessed: 2024-09-08.

R. M. Kinney, C. Anastasiades, R. Authur, I. Beltagy, and et al. J. Bragg. 2023. The semantic scholar open data platform. *ArXiv*, abs/2301.10140.

Robert W Lissitz and Joseph L Willhoft. 1985. A methodological study of the torrance tests of creativity. *Journal of Educational measurement*, 22(1):1–11.

Nelson F. Liu, Kevin Lin, John Hewitt, Ashwin Paranjape, Michele Bevilacqua, Fabio Petroni, and Percy Liang. 2024. Lost in the Middle: How Language Models Use Long Contexts. *Transactions of the Association for Computational Linguistics*, 12:157–173.

Li-Chun Lu, Shou-Jen Chen, Tsung-Min Pai, Chan-Hung Yu, Hung-yi Lee, and Shao-Hua Sun. 2024. LLM discussion: Enhancing the creativity of large language models via discussion framework and role-play. *CoRR*, abs/2405.06373.

Simone Luchini, Nadine T Maliakkal, Paul V DiStefano, John D Patterson, Roger Beaty, and Roni Reiter-Palmon. 2023. Automatic scoring of creative problem-solving with large language models: A comparison of originality and quality ratings.

Martha T Mednick and Sharon Halpern. 1968. Remote associates test. *Psychological Review*.

Sarnoff Mednick. 1962. The associative basis of the creative process. *Psychological review*, 69(3):220.

Pronita Mehrotra, Aishni Parab, and Sumit Gulwani. 2024. Enhancing creativity in large language models through associative thinking strategies. *CoRR*, abs/2405.06715.

Jay A Olson, Johnny Nahas, Denis Chmoulevitch, Simon J Cropper, and Margaret E Webb. 2021. Naming unrelated words predicts creativity. *Proceedings of the National Academy of Sciences*, 118(25):e2022340118.

OpenAI. 2023. GPT-4 technical report. *CoRR*, abs/2303.08774.

Peter Organisciak, Selcuk Acar, Denis Dumas, and Kelly Berthiaume. 2023. Beyond semantic distance: Automated scoring of divergent thinking greatly improves with large language models. *Thinking Skills and Creativity*, 49:101356.

William Orwig, Emma R Edenbaum, Joshua D Greene, and Daniel L Schacter. 2024. The language of creativity: Evidence from humans and large language models. *The Journal of creative behavior*, 58(1):128–136.

Antoine Bellemare Pépin, François Lespinasse, Philipp Thölke, Yann Harel, Kory Mathewson, Jay A. Olson, Yoshua Bengio, and Karim Jerbi. 2024. Divergent creativity in humans and large language models. *CoRR*, abs/2405.13012.

Matthew Renze and Erhan Guven. 2024. Self-reflection in llm agents: Effects on problem-solving performance. *Preprint*, arXiv:2405.06682.

M.A. Runco. 2011. Runco creativity assessment battery (rcab). *Creativity Testing Services.*

Mark A Runco and Garrett J Jaeger. 2012. The standard definition of creativity. *Creativity research journal*, 24(1):92–96.

Sotaro Shibayama, Deyun Yin, and Kuniko Matsumoto. 2021. Measuring novelty in science with word embedding. *PloS one*, 16(7):e0254034.

Chenglei Si, Diyi Yang, and Tatsunori Hashimoto. 2024. Can llms generate novel research ideas? a large-scale human study with 100+ nlp researchers. *arXiv preprint arXiv:2409.04109.*

Claire Stevenson, Iris Smal, Matthijs Baas, Raoul P. P. P. Grasman, and Han L. J. van der Maas. 2022. Putting gpt-3's creativity to the (alternative uses) test. In *Proceedings of the 13th International Conference on Computational Creativity, Bozen-Bolzano, Italy, June 27 - July 1, 2022*, pages 164–168. Association for Computational Creativity (ACC).

Marco Antonio Stranisci, Rossana Damiano, Enrico Mensa, Viviana Patti, Daniele Radicioni, and Tommaso Caselli. 2023. WikiBio: a semantic resource for the intersectional analysis of biographical events. In *Proceedings of the 61st Annual Meeting of the Association for Computational Linguistics (Volume 1: Long Papers)*, pages 12370–12384, Toronto, Canada. Association for Computational Linguistics.

Douglas Summers-Stay, Clare R Voss, and Stephanie M Lukin. 2023. Brainstorm, then select: a generative language model improves its creativity score. In *The AAAI-23 Workshop on Creative AI Across Modalities.*

Xuezhi Wang, Jason Wei, Dale Schuurmans, Quoc V. Le, Ed H. Chi, Sharan Narang, Aakanksha Chowdhery, and Denny Zhou. 2023. Self-consistency improves chain of thought reasoning in language models. In *The Eleventh International Conference on Learning Representations, ICLR 2023, Kigali, Rwanda, May 1-5, 2023*. OpenReview.net.

Jason Wei, Xuezhi Wang, Dale Schuurmans, Maarten Bosma, Brian Ichter, Fei Xia, Ed Chi, Quoc Le, and Denny Zhou. 2023. Chain-of-thought prompting elicits reasoning in large language models. *Preprint*, arXiv:2201.11903.

Xinyi Yan, Chengxi Luo, Charles L. A. Clarke, Nick Craswell, Ellen M. Voorhees, and Pablo Castells. 2022. Human preferences as dueling bandits. In *Proceedings of the 45th International ACM SIGIR Conference on Research and Development in Information Retrieval*, SIGIR '22, page 567–577, New York, NY, USA. Association for Computing Machinery.

Yunpu Zhao, Rui Zhang, Wenyi Li, Di Huang, Jiaming Guo, Shaohui Peng, Yifan Hao, Yuanbo Wen, Xing Hu, Zidong Du, Qi Guo, Ling Li, and Yunji Chen. 2024. Assessing and understanding creativity in large language models. *CoRR*, abs/2401.12491.

A Appendix

A.1 Statistics of arXiv

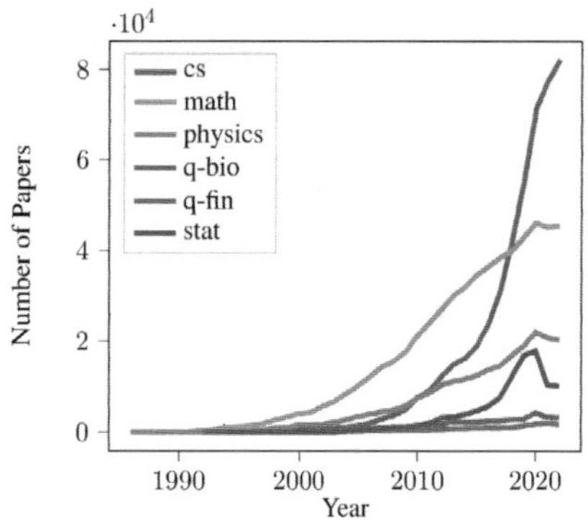

Figure 6: Number of Papers for Each Field (Up to 2023)

A.2 Zero-shot

You will be provided with the title and abstract of two research papers. Please determine which of the two articles is more novel. Follow these steps for evaluation.

Step 1: Identify the problem and solution that the research paper attempts to solve.

Step 2: Determine how unique the solution is given the current research landscape in 2024. Does the paper introduce a new idea, theory, or concept that has not been previously discussed in the literature?

Step 3: Determine how creative the solution is given the current research landscape in 2024. Does it apply a known idea in a completely new context or in a way that has not been done before?

Step 4: Using the findings from Steps 1-3, determine which paper is more novel.

In your response, please only state which paper is more novel (e.g., 1 if Paper 1 is more novel; 2 if Paper 2 is more novel).

User Prompt:

- Paper 1 Title: [paper_1_title]
- Paper 1 Abstract: [paper_1_abstract]
- Paper 2 Title: [paper_2_title]
- Paper 2 Abstract: [paper_2_abstract]

A.3 Self-Reflection

You are an advanced language model tasked with determining the novelty of research papers in 2024. Your goal is to evaluate and compare the novelty of two research papers based on their titles, abstracts, and any other given metadata.
The order in which the papers are presented is random and should not influence your evaluation.
Step 1: Independent Evaluation
Analyze each research paper's title and abstract **independently**. Treat each paper as if it is the only one under review at that moment.
Consider the following aspects for each paper:

- **Novelty of Methodology**: Are the methods used new and innovative?
- **Surprisingness of Findings**: Are the findings unexpected or counterintuitive?
- **Impact on Existing Knowledge**: How does the research challenge or expand current scientific understanding?
- **Potential for Future Research**: Does the paper open up new directions for research?
- **Relevance to 2024 Scientific Understanding**: How well does the paper align with or push the boundaries of current trends?

Step 2: Quantitative Assessment

- Assign a score from 1-10 to each research paper for its novelty, with 10 being the most novel. This score should be based solely on the content of the title and abstract.
- Provide a brief justification for the score, using specific quotes and context.

Step 3: Final Comparison

- After independently scoring each paper, compare the scores.
- Determine which paper exhibits greater novelty based on the higher score, and provide the identifier (X or Y) of the more novel paper.

Important: The order of presentation is random and should not influence your decision. Evaluate each paper strictly on its content and merit.

User Prompt:

- Paper X Title: [paper_x_title]
- Paper X Abstract: [paper_x_abstract]
- Paper Y Title: [paper_y_title]
- Paper Y Abstract: [paper_y_abstract]

A.4 SchNovel

Algorithm 1 Data Sampling Algorithm

```
Fields ← [cs, math, physics, qbio, qfin, stat]
startYear ← [2019, 2020, 2021, 2022, 2023]
yearGap ← [2, 4, 6, 8, 10]
sampleNum ← 100
N ← 0
Dataset ← []
for f in Fields do
    for s in startYear do
        for g in yearGap do
            while N ≠ sampleNum do
                x ← paper published in s from f
                y ← paper published in s-g from f
                label ← x
                Dataset ← (f, g, s, x, y, label)
                N ← N + 1
            end while
            N ← 0
        end for
    end for
end for
```

A.5 LLM Discussion

You are a [Role] with expertise across all areas of [Category]. You will be provided with the titles and abstracts of two research papers. Your task is to determine which of the two articles is more novel by evaluating their originality, contribution to the field, and potential impact. Focus on aspects such as new methodologies, unexplored problems, innovative solutions, and how the work advances the state of the art. Follow these steps for evaluation.

Step 1: Identify the problem and solution that the research paper attempts to solve.

Step 2: Determine how unique the solution is given the current research landscape in 2024. Does the paper introduce a new idea, theory, or concept that has not been previously discussed in the literature?

Step 3: Determine how creative the solution is given the current research landscape in 2024. Does it apply a known idea in a completely new context or in a way that has not been done before?

Step 4: Using the findings from Steps 1-3, determine which paper is more novel.

Please limit your response to 150 tokens max. In your response please conclude with: "The more novel and impactful paper is [Paper X or Paper Y]

User Prompt:

- Paper X Title: [paper_x_title]
- Paper X Abstract: [paper_x_abstract]
- Paper Y Title: [paper_y_title]
- Paper Y Abstract: [paper_y_abstract]
- *(Round 2 Discussion add on)* [previous_response] These are responses from other reviewers. Please revise your response if necessary... [other_responses]
- *(Round 3 Discussion add on)* These are responses from other reviewers. Please determine which paper is more novel... [other_responses]

A.6 RAG-Novelty

You are an advanced language model tasked with determining the novelty of research papers in 2024. Your goal is to evaluate and compare the novelty of two research papers based on their titles and abstracts.
The order in which the papers are presented is random and should not influence your evaluation.
Step 1: Independent Evaluation
Analyze each research paper's title and abstract **independently**. Treat each paper as if it is the only one under review at that moment.
Retrieve similar abstracts from a vector database based on the provided abstracts.
Contextual Date Analysis: Average the published dates of the retrieved documents. Use this average date as additional context for your evaluation. Consider that papers with an average date that is later or more recent in time are generally more novel.
Consider the following aspects for each paper:

- **Novelty of Methodology:** Are the methods used new and innovative?
- **Surprisingness of Findings:** Are the findings unexpected or counterintuitive?
- **Impact on Existing Knowledge:** How does the research challenge or expand current scientific understanding?
- **Potential for Future Research:** Does the paper open up new directions for research?
- **Relevance to 2024 Scientific Understanding:** How well does the paper align with or push the boundaries of current trends?

Step 2: Quantitative Assessment

- Assign a score from 1-10 to each research paper for its novelty, with 10 being the most novel. This score should be based on the content of the title and abstract, as well as the contextual information from the average published dates.
- Provide a brief justification for the score, using specific quotes and context.

Step 3: Final Comparison

- After independently scoring each paper, compare the scores.
- Determine which paper exhibits greater novelty based on the higher score, and conclude with: "The more novel and impactful paper is [Paper X or Paper Y].

Important: The order of presentation is random and should not influence your decision. Evaluate each paper strictly on its content and merit, incorporating the additional context from the vector database as described.

User Prompt:

- Paper X Average Cosine Similarity: [paper_x_avg_cosine_similarity]
- Paper X Average Contextual Date: [paper_x_avg_contextual_date]
- Paper Y Average Cosine Similarity: [paper_y_avg_cosine_similarity]
- Paper Y Average Contextual Date: [paper_y_avg_contextual_date]
- Paper X Title: [paper_x_title]
- Paper X Abstract: [paper_x_abstract]
- Paper Y Title: [paper_y_title]
- Paper Y Abstract: [paper_y_abstract]

LLM-Assisted Translation of Legacy FORTRAN Codes to C++: A Cross-Platform Study

Nishath Rajiv Ranasinghe[1], Shawn M. Jones[1], Michal Kucer[1], Ayan Biswas[1], Daniel O'Malley[1], Alexander Buschmann Most[1], Selma Liliane Wanna[1], Ajay Sreekumar[2]
[1]Los Alamos National Laboratory, Los Alamos NM 87545,
[2]School of Information, University of Arizona, 103 E 2nd St 4, Tucson, AZ 85721
Correspondence: ayan@lanl.gov

Abstract

Large Language Models (LLMs) are increasingly being leveraged for generating and translating scientific computer codes by both domain-experts and non-domain experts. Fortran has served as one of the go to programming languages in legacy high-performance computing (HPC) for scientific discoveries. Despite growing adoption, LLM-based code translation of legacy code-bases has not been thoroughly assessed or quantified for its usability. Here, we studied the applicability of LLM-based translation of Fortran to C++ as a step towards building an agentic-workflow using open-weight LLMs on two different computational platforms. We statistically quantified the compilation accuracy of the translated C++ codes, measured the similarity of the LLM translated code to the human translated C++ code, and statistically quantified the output similarity of the Fortran to C++ translation.

1 Introduction

A Large volume of scientific computational software implemented in HPC environments has been written in programming languages such as Fortran and C due to their superior performance. However, recent advancements in computer hardware are not fully utilized by older generations of Fortran, and these legacy codes often encounter difficulties with memory allocations. There is a lack of human resources to maintain and improve these code-bases for mission critical applications in the future (Shipman and Randles, 2023; Pietrini et al., 2024).

Propriety (e.g. ChatGPT) and open weight (e.g. Llama (Touvron et al., 2023)) LLMs have vastly improved code generation (Wang and Chen, 2023) and code translation between modern programming languages (Jiao et al., 2023) due to widespread availability of training examples, but not without difficulties (Pan et al., 2024). As efforts expand to translate scientific software from legacy programming languages to more modern languages via agentic workflows, there is a need for systematic methods to evaluate the effectiveness of machine generated scientific software.

However, very few studies exist for LLM-assisted code translation from Fortran to C++, primarily due to a lack of quality training data sets. A recent study (Lei et al., 2023), compiled pairs of OpenMP Fortran and equivalent C++ codes to evaluate LLM code translation and evaluated their results using both quantitative (e.g., CodeBLEU score (Ren et al., 2020)) and qualitative approaches (e.g., human evaluation). There is also a lack of LLM-based Fortran to C++ code translation tools that can be readily deployed to assist developers in mission critical and secure environments. Furthermore, earlier attempts to translate code from Fortran to C++ have not accounted for successful compiles or output evaluation of the translated code (Theurich et al., 2001).

In this study, we make several contributions. We conduct an analysis of translating open-source code-bases using open-weight models. Our workflow (Figure 1) is designed to be agnostic of any specific LLM or computational platform (e.g., vLLM), building towards a set of standardized evaluation measures for machine-generated code translation. We evaluate the similarity to the human-translated target code using the common CodeBLEU measure (Ren et al., 2020), how much of the translated code compiles (compilation accuracy (Wen et al., 2022a)), and how well the output of the compiled translated code matches the original compiled Fortran code (output similarity). We also categorize any compile errors to demonstrate different behaviors among LLMs. To our knowledge, this is the first attempt to statistically quantify code translation accuracies of open-weight LLMs between computational platforms, the first such study involving Fortran, and the first to apply all of these evaluation techniques together.

Proceedings of the 1st Workshop on AI and Scientific Discovery: Directions and Opportunities, pages 58–69
May 3, 2025

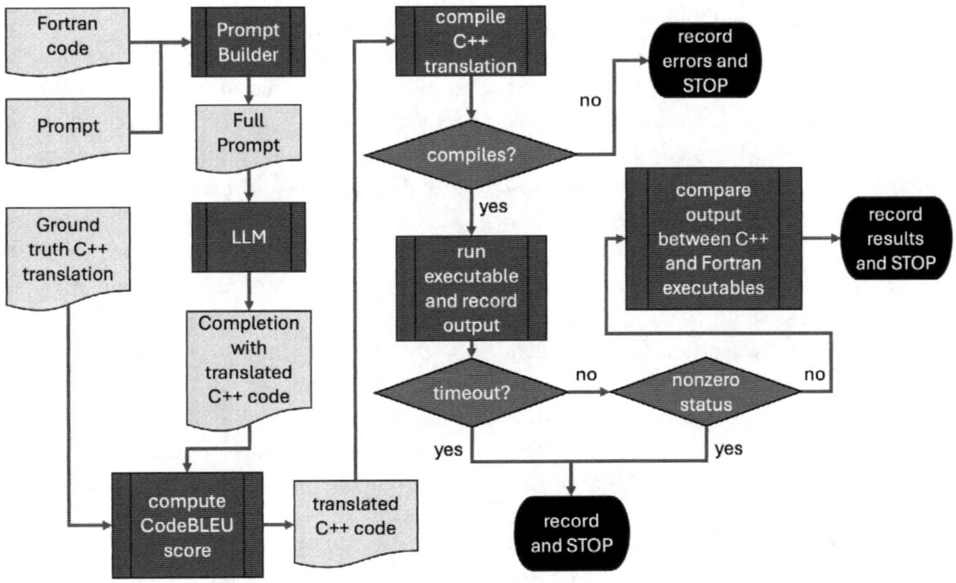

Figure 1: Regardless of LLM, our workflow evaluates several parts of the LLM's code translation, starting by comparing it to a human-translated ground truth with CodeBLEU, then moving to evaluate how well the translation compiles and executes. Finally, the workflow compares the output between the original Fortran code and the translated code's C++ executable.

2 Background

Despite the emergence of numerous modern programming languages, Fortran remains integral in legacy scientific applications, HPC, and areas requiring intensive numerical computations, such as climate modeling (Méndez et al., 2014), computational fluid dynamics (Derlaga et al., 2013), solving inverse problems (Cuer and Bayer, 1980), full waveform inversion (Komatitsch and Tromp, 2002), subsurface flow (Mills et al., 2007), space applications (Ocampo and Senent, 2006), crystallography (Grosse-Kunstleve et al., 2002), radiation transport (Waters et al., 2007) and structural analysis (Nardelli, 1995). Unfortunately, Fortran is no longer a popular language (Shipman and Randles, 2023) and finding assistance from the community for future development is challenging. We chose C++ as a target language because it has more community support, but it also has a number of desirable features for scientific computing in the HPC environment, including its highly efficient feature set, template techniques (Veldhuizen and Jernigan, 1997), the standard template library (Musser and Saini, 1995), and advanced memory management (Attardi et al., 1998). Unfortunately, efforts to translate legacy code-bases from Fortran to C++ have encountered several challenges stemming from differences in language paradigms, syntax, and standard libraries.

LLMs have emerged as an efficient and robust method for translating code between programming languages. Many LLMs exist (de Groot, 2024), and there are different computational platforms (Emani et al., 2022) for executing LLMs. In this work, we evaluate two such platforms: vLLM and SambaNova. vLLM is a library providing a common interface for efficiently serving different LLMs across different hardware architectures utilizing the PagedAttention algorithm (Kwon et al., 2023). SambaNova is an AI accelerator platform that provides specialized hardware for executing LLMs (Prabhakar et al., 2024). We compare both in this paper.

3 Related Work

Fortran to C++ translation has traditionally been conducted manually by experienced programmers. There have been few efforts to convert these legacy code-bases from Fortran to C++ using source-to-source translation tools (Grosse-Kunstleve et al., 2012; Feldman, 1990). However, the translated codes from these sources lack readability and require manual changes to implement memory management functionality (Theurich et al., 2001).

Previous systematic studies of code translation between pairs of modern programming languages such as C, C++, Go, Java, and Python using LLMs have been met with varying degree of compilation success from 2.1 to 47.3% for code specific (codeGEN, CodeGenX, StarCoder) and text based general purpose (GPT-4, Llama-2, TB-Airboros, TB-Vicuna) LLMs with GPT-4 having the most success (Pan et al., 2024). Recent efforts to create larger code bases of example training data sets for popular and niche programming languages have improved the LLM assisted translations between more modern languages (Yan et al., 2023). A recent study (Chen et al., 2024) utilized an LLM based agentic method that seamlessly integrates multiple verification processes into iterative cycles for translating Fortran to C++. This approach employs a questioner-solver module to delegate referencing and decision-making tasks to separate LLMs, a multi-turn dialogue collection that effectively captures the nuanced aspects of translating and finally fine-tuning of three open-weight LLMs using the data produced to improve the accuracy of the models. Our study differs from theirs (Chen et al., 2024) by evaluating the capabilities of open-weight LLMs that can be readily deployed in a mission critical environment to translate Fortran to C++ on different computational architectures. We also differ by our choice in evaluations. We include compilation accuracy, the translated code's similarity to human translated codes, and a comparison of the similarity of outputs between our ground truth Fortran codes and the translated code from the LLM. Unlike other studies, we also apply the open-source Rosetta code repository (Rosetta Code Community, 2025) as a data source for evaluating the translation of Fortran to C++.

4 Methodology

4.1 Data

To evaluate how well each LLM's translation matches a human translation, we required not only Fortran code, but ground truth C++ translations. We acquired two datasets containing pairs of Fortran and equivalent C++ codes. Rosetta Code (Rosetta Code Community, 2025) provides coding examples for the same programming task in multiple languages. We created a web scraper to produce a dataset of 243 Fortran and their corresponding C++ examples from the Rosetta Code website in October 2023. We retained only those examples for which there was at least one Fortran and corresponding C++ example per programming task. Our second dataset consists of 101 examples from the DataRaceBench (DRB) benchmark (Liao et al., 2017) obtained from the OpenMP Fortran to C++ dataset (Lei et al., 2023) that contains the same code implemented in different languages in support of the benchmark. From each dataset, we selected fully developed 344 computer programs with varying degrees of complexity, to ensure ground truth Fortran and C++ programs compile.

4.2 LLMs

Model parameters in LLMs are preset configurations that determine the model's architecture and training process, such as the number of layers, learning rate, and batch size. The number of parameters varies between LLMs. However, prior work (Hoffmann et al., 2022) demonstrated that the performance of LLMs does not necessarily linearly increase with the number of parameters.

We chose LLMs that are well regarded by industry, can be deployed in a mission-critical environment, allow for local deployment to satisfy privacy concerns, have a diversity of model parameter sizes for comparison, and are also supported by the vLLM and SambaNova Cloud platforms (SambaNova). Table 1 shows the LLMs we selected based on this criteria.

4.3 Workflow

Figure 1 shows the evaluation process we applied to each Fortran code and LLM. We start by building each full prompt by combining each Fortran code with the prompt in Figure 2. Using this full prompt, we requested that each LLM convert the Fortran code to C++. Because LLMs are known to vary their responses due to their stochastic nature, we issued the same prompt multiple times for each Fortran code. We set up vLLM (Kwon et al., 2023) using onsite hardware at the Los Alamos National Laboratory (DGX hardware equipped with 8 A100s NVIDIA GPUs along with 2 AMD EPYC 7742 64-Core Processors) and issued the same prompt 128 times per Fortran code per LLM. We utilized temperature of 0.8, min-p of 0.05, top-p of 0.95, and set the maximum generation length to 8192 tokens across the LLM models. We also used the OpenAI Python API library to prompt Llama models hosted by SambaNova Cloud, which is equipped with SambaNova SN40 Reconfigurable Dataflow Units (RDUs) (Prabhakar et al., 2024). Due to rate limits on the SambaNova Cloud, we only executed the same prompt 25 times per Fortran code

Table 1: The LLMs used in this study.

LLM	# parameters	Computational platform
Open code interpreter	33B	vLLM
Llama 3.1	70B	vLLM
Mistral Large Instruct 2407	123B	vLLM
Llama 3.3	70B	vLLM
Llama 3.1	8B	SambaNova Cloud
Llama 3.1	70B	SambaNova Cloud
Llama 3.1	405B	SambaNova Cloud
Llama 3.3	70B	SambaNova Cloud

```
You are an exceptionally intelligent coding assistant specializing in code
translation, particularly from Fortran to C++. You consistently deliver accurate
and reliable translations while maintaining the original code's functionality and
structure.

Please translate this Fortran code to C++. Follow these guidelines:
1. Maintain the overall structure and functionality of the original code.
2. Use modern C++ practices and idioms where appropriate.
3. Ensure that all functions, subroutines, and modules are properly translated to
their C++ equivalents.
4. Pay attention to differences in array handling, I/O operations, and memory
management between Fortran and C++.
5. Include any necessary C++ libraries or headers.
6. Add comments to explain any significant changes or non-trivial translations.

Please return the translated C++ code in one code block.
Please restrict your output to the translated code only.
```

Figure 2: The prompt used in this study.

per LLM. We utilized temperature of 0.8, top-p of 0.9, and context length of 4096 across the Llama models in the SambaNova Cloud. From each completion, we recorded the C++ code and compared it to the ground truth C++ code from our datasets via CodeBLEU score (Ren et al., 2020). From there, we evaluated the Fortran code's compilation accuracy and output similarity.

4.4 Similarity to human translated code

CodeBLEU (Ren et al., 2020) measures how well a machine translation matches a human translation for the same code. The CodeBLEU score contains four dimensions of comparison: matching n-grams, matching weighted n-grams, Abstract Syntax Tree matching, and data-flow analysis. We apply the human ground truth translation from each dataset to arrive at a CodeBLEU score. We perform bias analysis of the translated C++ codes across various LLMs, as an indicator of the code translation quality. We use CodeBLEU scores of the human translated C++ codes with their corresponding machine translated codes. In our scenario, since we run the same translation command prompt for a given code multiple times and we might get variations in the code translation, our bias analysis takes into account this stochasticity in LLM-based code generation. To perform this, for each LLM, we first calculate individual average CodeBLEU scores for each ground truth Fortran file across the trials. Since CodeBLEU depicts similarity, we calculate bias (that represents error) as $Bias = 1 - CodeBLEU$. With this formulation, now we can use these averaged bias scores to approximate a distribution using a non-parametric Kernel Density Estimate (KDE) approach(Chen, 2017). In this method, there exist different choices for its kernel types; such as Gaussian, triangular, rectangular, and the Epanechnikov kernel (Gramacki, 2018). Generally, variations due to kernel types are considered to be less significant compared to the choice of kernel bandwidth (Silverman, 1998). Silverman's rule of thumb for bandwidth selection generally produces smooth and good-quality density estimation (Biswas et al., 2016). We use this approach in our work and generate the KDE plots, as shown in Figure 3a for vLLM based translated codes and Figure 3b shows the KDE plots for the SambaNova Cloud based translated codes.

Table 2: Classification of compiler errors used in this work.

Compile Error Category	Error topic	String matches from g++ compiler
Syntax Error	Missing operators, missing delimiters, incorrect usage of tokens, or anything else resulting from poor programming syntax	expected before error: no match for 'operator>= stray '' in program error: void value not ignored as it ought to be error: 'std::std' has not been declaredcannot be used as a function error: assignment of read-only locationerror: invalid initialization of non-const reference of type error: lvalue required as increment operand error: no matching function for call to error: missing terminating " character error: too many arguments to function
Type Error	An issue with use of data types	invalid conversion cannot convert
Linker Error	The implied use of external libraries	is not a member of 'std' error: aggregate 'std::stringstream ss' has incomplete type and cannot be defined undefined reference
Declaration Error	Declaring variables before use	error: too many initializers was not declared has not been declared
Semantic Error	Proper application of functions or operators	invalid operands invalid use of
Scope Error	Using variable outside of their established scope	not in this scope is not captured
Template Error	Invalid use of C++ templates	wrong number of template arguments
File and I/O Error	the code refers to nonexistent filesystem resources	No such file or directory
Memory Error	Incorrect use of memory operations	invalid use of delete
Other Error	Anything else not covered with the string matching above	

4.5 Success of compilation

Compilation accuracy of the translated C++ measures how many translations successfully compile without errors (Wen et al., 2022b). We compiled each translated C++ using the g++ v5.3.0 compiler on Red Hat Enterprise Linux Workstation release 7.9. If a C++ translation failed to compile, we recorded the compiler output and did not proceed further with that translation (Figure 1). We reviewed the compiler output and categorized each error as shown in Table 2. The

4.6 Similarity of outputs

Output similarity compares the output of each Fortran program to that of its C++ translation generated from the LLM. We compiled each Fortran program and ran the resulting executable to capture its output. Then, we did the same with each LLM-generated C++ translation that successfully compiled. Outputs from scientific programs consist of text and numeric data. Humans may look at two outputs and consider them the same where a direct string match would score them radically different (e.g., `b(50,50)= 0.00000000` vs. `b(50,50)= 0.0` and `Fib for 30 832040` vs. `Fib for 30 = 832040.0`). We first tokenized each output using the NLTK (Bird et al., 2009) `word_tokenize` function to produce a list of strings. Then, we attempted to convert each token to a floating point number using the Python `float` function. If the token could be converted, we rounded it to a precision of 4 decimal places. If not, then we left the token as a string. We, then applied a Jaro-Winkler (Jaro, 1989; Winkler, 1990) score to each set of tokens to measure their similarity.

Thus, by the end of the workflow we have evaluated each translation in comparison to a human translation, how well it compiles, and whether it produces the same output as the Fortran submitted to the system at the beginning.

5 Results and Discussion

5.1 Similarity to human translated code

CodeBLEU scores demonstrate how well an LLM's code translation matches a human translation of the same code. Figure 3 shows the bias of CodeBLEU scores between LLMs. Scores on the x-axis provide a distance between LLM generated C++ translations and their human ground truth equivalents. Higher scores that indicate that the translation is farther than the ground truth and thus a poorer match. At first glance Figure 3 appears to show that there is not much difference between LLMs, but the peaks give a more nuanced story.

Figure 3a shows that Llama 3.1 70B leads with the highest rate of translations that do not match human ground truth. OpenCodeInterpreter 33B

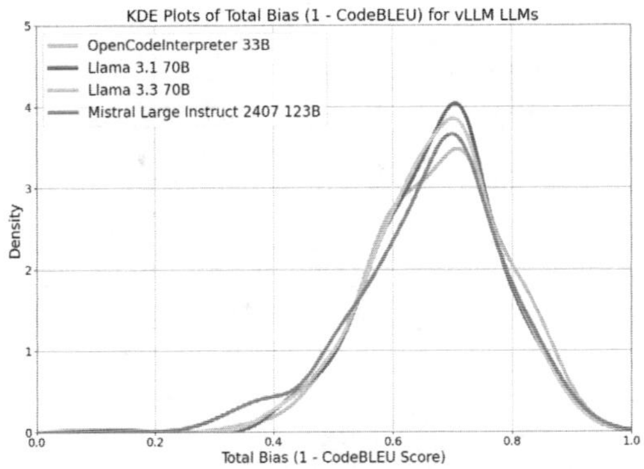

(a) vLLM

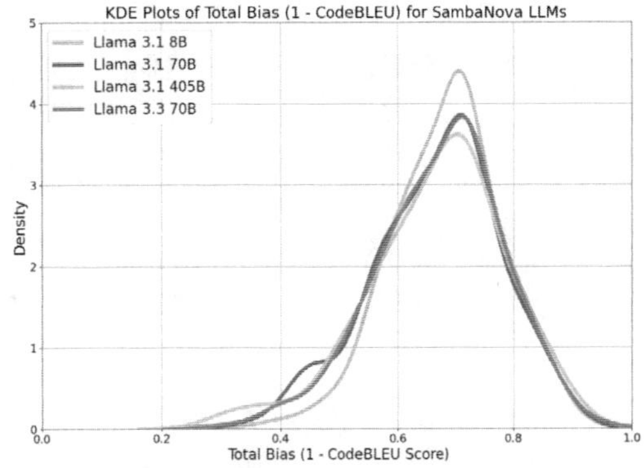

(b) SambaNova

Figure 3: Kernel density estimate plots demonstrating the distribution of total bias (1 - CodeBLEU Score) for each Fortran translation demonstrates different distributions per execution platform.

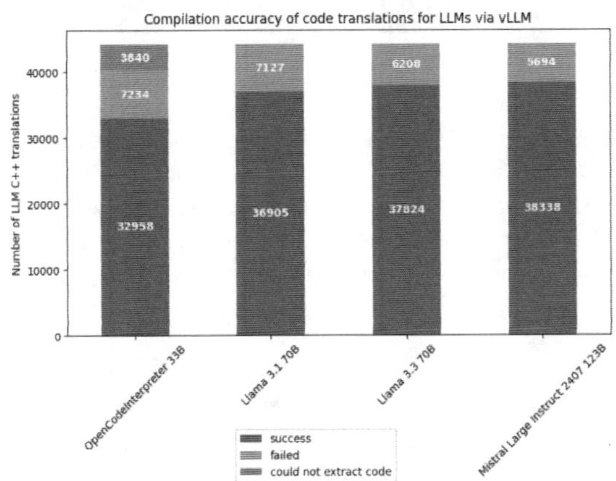

(a) vLLM

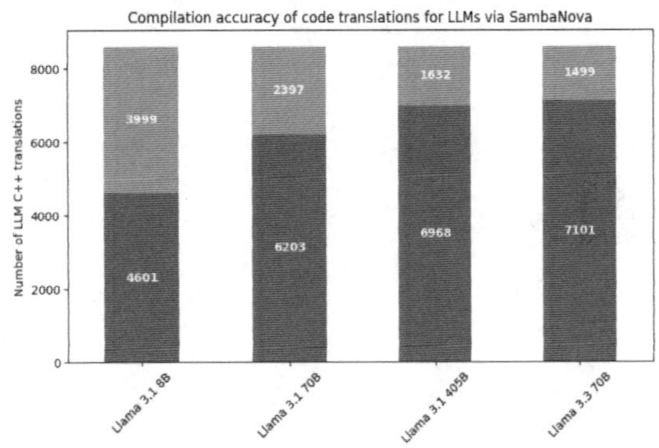

(b) SambaNova

Figure 4: Compilation accuracy of each LLM by execution platform shows that the increase in the number of model parameters is proportional to the increase in compilation accuracy.

(Zheng et al., 2025) has the lowest peak outperforming Mistral Large. However, Mistral does have a small peak lower on the x-axis, indicating many more that might be closer to human ground truth.

SambaNova has a similar peak in Figure 3b, indicating a higher number of LLM translations that do not match human ground truth. Llama 3.1 8B's CodeBLEU bias is highest. Thus, its translations are least consistent with human translations. In contrast, Llama 3.1 405B has the lowest peak, but appears only marginally better in consistency than other models. These results with the commonly-used CodeBLEU metric demonstrate that larger models provide translations closer to human ground truth, but the amount of similarity in these distributions necessitate our other measures to more clearly separate performance.

5.2 Success of compilation

Figure 4 shows the compilation accuracy results for each computational platform and LLM. In both cases, we see an increase in the number of successful compiles as one increases the number of parameters in the LLM. Additionally, as seen in Figure 4a, while the LLMs served by vLLM appear to generate more successfully compilable code, OpenCodeInterpreter generates completions from which we cannot extract code. In contrast, SambaNova's results in Figure 4b show no instances where LLM completions produced code that could not be extracted. Additionally, we see that, for vLLM, Llama 3.1 70B and Llama 3.3 70B have comparable performance. This is not the case with these two LLMs on SambaNova Cloud, where Llama 3.1 405B and Llama 3.3 70B have similar performance.

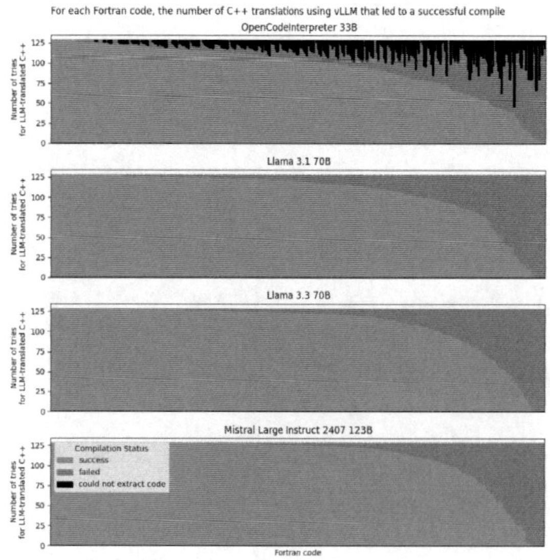

(a) vLLM

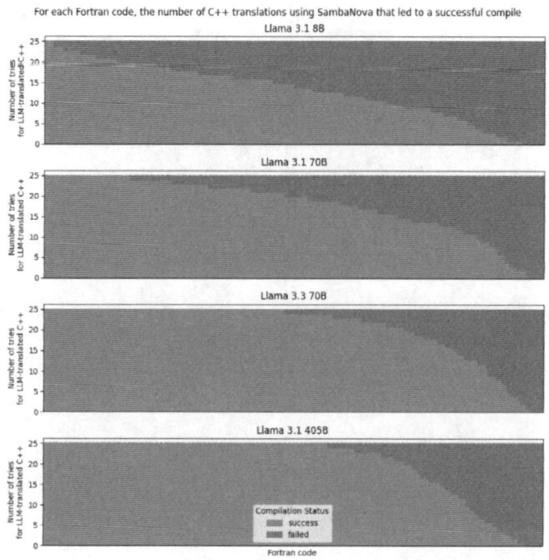

(b) SambaNova

Figure 5: Each Fortran code is plotted along the x-axis while the count of tries for a corresponding C++ translation is placed on the y-axis. Translations that compiled successfully are shown in green, and those that failed are marked in red. Note same Fortran code is not always shown at the same point in the x-axis. Compilation accuracy of each translated Fortran program differs per model with some LLMs having more difficulty translating certain codes than others. We note that LLMs with a higher number of parameters have more success per Fortran code.

Figure 5 demonstrates the distribution of compilation accuracy for all Fortran codes. These sand-charts represent each Fortran code on the x-axis. The y-axis represents each translation of that code into C++. Green shows translations that successfully compile. Red shows failures. By executing each LLM multiple times we can see the level of variation in their responses and note that not all translation failures occurred equally. Some translations were always successfully compiled while others were more varied. We also note the same pattern of improving compilation accuracy among all Fortran codes as the number of parameters increases across models. vLLM shows more consistent translations (green rising closer to the top) while SambaNova shows a dramatic improvement for Llama 3.1 405B over Llama 3.3 70B that was not apparent in the raw numbers shown in Figure 5b.

Figure 6 shows the distribution and categorization of of compile failures. In Figure 6a, most of the compile errors generated from the LLMs served in vLLM are linker errors, representing the assumed inclusion of libraries not specified via an `#include` directive. In contrast, in Figure 6b the majority of the compile errors shown for LLMs served in SambaNova Cloud are syntax errors. Again, we see that Llama 3.3 70B and Llama 3.1 405B have comparable performance, though their compile error distribution varies.

5.3 Similarity of outputs

Figure 7 shows the distribution of Jaro-Winkler scores comparing the outputs of the ground truth Fortran programs to the outputs of their LLM C++ translations. We note the same familiar pattern of increasing number of parameters leads to better mean similarity of inputs. Mistral Large with vLLM in Figure 7a and Llama 3.1 405B with SambaNova in Figure 7b both outperform Llama 3.3 70B in this case. Mistral Large, however produces a tighter distribution of similar outputs.

6 Conclusion

We conducted an analysis of how well open-weight LLMs translate open-source code-bases from Fortran to C++. We presented an LLM-independent and platform-independent workflow for our evaluation. This workflow evaluates several elements of translation quality. We consider the similarity between human ground truth and machine translation, if the translated C++ code compiles, what errors are encountered if the compile fails, and finally how well the resulting C++ translation's ex-

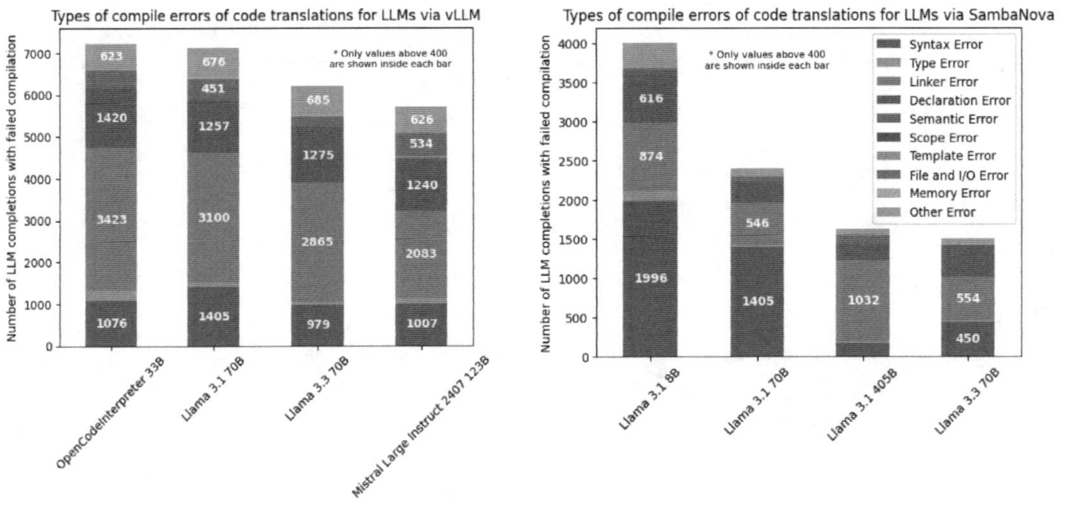

(a) vLLM

(b) SambaNova

Figure 6: Distribution of compile error categories for each C++ translation shows that LLMs produce different errors in their translated code.

ecutable produces the same output as the original Fortran code.

We ran this workflow with LLMs on both the vLLM and SambaNova Cloud platforms. Because LLMs do not always produce the same output each time, we ran 128 instances of the same translation on vLLM and 25 on SambaNova to ensure we had a sizeable sample space. Unsurprisingly, we discovered that those LLMs with higher model parameter counts tend to produce better results. Our codeBLEU analysis reveals that Mistral Large served on vLLM and Llama 3.1 405B served on SambaNova Cloud produce codes that better matches human translations. Our compilation evaluation demonstrates that Mistral Large on vLLM and Llama 3.1 405B on SamaNova Cloud have higher counts of compilable code, with Llama-3.3 70B being comparable. We demonstrated that not all Fortran codes were translated consistently, showing that some LLMs produced C++ translations that more consistently compiled for a given Fortran code. We also found that the translated codes from vLLM that failed to compile mostly had linker errors while those from SambaNova largely contained syntax errors, even for the same LLM model. Finally, we showed that, for successful compiles, the output of the translated executables better matched the output of the original Fortran with Mistral Large on vLLM and Llama 3.1 405B on SambaNova Cloud, with Llama 3.3 70B being comparable on both platforms.

The implications for scientific computing are mixed. The state of the art shows the code bases in Fortran can be translated to C++ readily, but also demonstrate that no LLM on either platform was free of error. We still require a human-in-the-loop for code translation.

7 Limitations

While our study presents a workflow for systematic evaluation of open-weight LLMs for Fortran-to-C++ code translation, there are several limitations that must be acknowledged: Our evaluation workflow is not yet packaged into a standalone tool that can provide Fortran-to-C++ translations along with compilation statistics and output similarity. Automating this workflow would make scientific discovery more accessible for researchers working in HPC environments. We did not present our attempts to improve compilation accuracy through agentic workflows by incorporating the error messages generated from compiling the codes produced by the LLM into a automatic dialog with the LLM. Our initial efforts in that direction were shown to increase the compilation accuracies of the translated codes and we are pursuing the agentic workflows in a future study.

Additionally, our study could be enhanced by incorporating more complex and extensive Fortran code-bases, such John Burkardt's data set (Burkardt, Accessed: 2025-01-30) which are highly

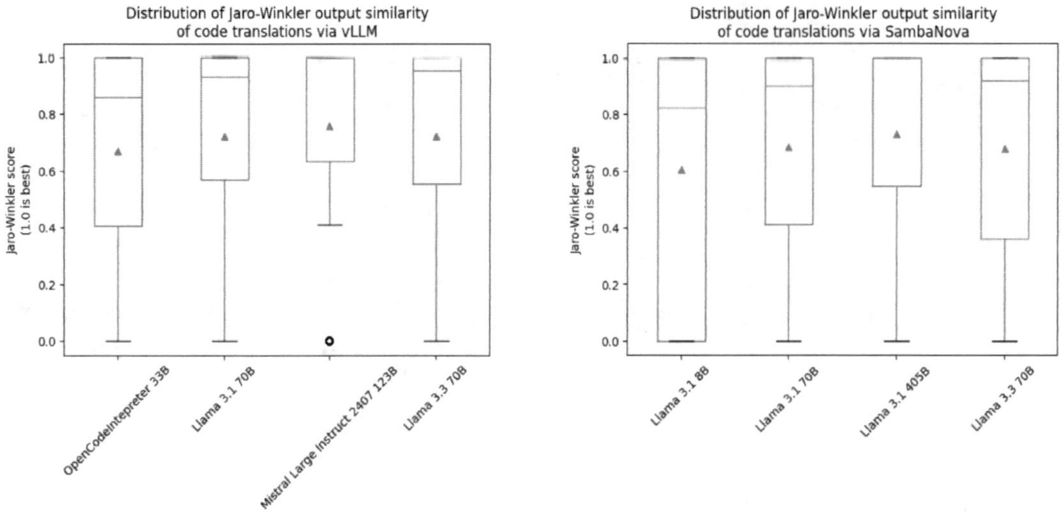

(a) vLLM

(b) SambaNova

Figure 7: Distribution of Jaro-Winkler scores for output similarity comparison between original Fortran executables and LLM C++ executables. Green triangles represent means while green lines are medians.

relevant to scientific computing. Furthermore, Chen et al. (Chen et al., 2024) showed that fine-tuning LLMs on Fortran to C++ datasets could improve each model's CodeBLEU scores by 1.5 to 3.3 times with up to a 92% increase in successful compilations. Focusing our study's analysis on models which have been fine-tuned for Fortran to C++ translation could help create more useful tools for developers.

Further improvements could be made with prompt design and in this study, we used the same prompt for every LLM. It is possible that further exploration of prompt design could uncover that different models perform better with different prompts (Liu et al., 2023; Knobloch et al., 2025). Our study focused solely on open-weight LLMs such as Llama and Mistral. While comparisons do exist for both natural language translation as well as coding (without translating), our literature review found a lack of studies comparing open-weight LLMs to proprietary models like GPT and Gemini for code translation. Including these models, along with the source-to-source translation tools (Feldman, 1990; Grosse-Kunstleve et al., 2012) which were popular for Fortran to C++ in the past could provide a clearer benchmark for our results. Additionally, in this study, we did not test the capabilities of the new generation of reasoning models (OpenAI's o1, o1-mini, o3-mini; DeepSeek-R1; and Anthropic Claude 3.7 Sonnet) to translate Fortran to C++. However, our workflow delivers a plug-and-play solution to test any LLMs code translation capabilities on any computational platform without any modifications.

In this study, we did not consider improving code translation accuracy using few-shot learning via Retrieval Augmented Generation (RAG) as it is studied elsewhere (Bhattarai et al., 2024).

8 Acknowledgments

This work was supported by the Computational Systems and Software Environments subprogram of National Nuclear Security Administration's (NNSA's) Advanced Simulation and Computing program through Los Alamos National Laboratory (LANL). LANL is operated by Triad National Security, LLC, for the National Nuclear Security Administration of U.S. Department of Energy (Contract No. 89233218CNA000001). This research used resources provided by the Darwin testbed and DGX pod at LANL which is funded by the Computational Systems and Software Environments subprogram of LANL's Advanced Simulation and Computing program (NNSA/DOE). We are also grateful to SambaNova Systems, Inc for providing access to SambaNova Cloud and technical support. This work is approved for unlimited release with an LA-UR number LA-UR-25-22376.

References

Giuseppe Attardi, Tito Flagella, and Pietro Iglio. 1998. A customisable memory management framework for c++. *Software: Practice and Experience*, 28(11):1143–1184.

Manish Bhattarai, Javier E. Santos, Shawn Jones, Ayan Biswas, Boian Alexandrov, and Daniel O'Malley. 2024. Enhancing code translation in language models with few-shot learning via retrieval-augmented generation. *Preprint*, arXiv:2407.19619.

Steven Bird, Ewan Klein, and Edward Loper. 2009. *Natural language processing with Python: analyzing text with the natural language toolkit.* " O'Reilly Media, Inc.".

Ayan Biswas, Guang Lin, Xiaotong Liu, and Han-Wei Shen. 2016. Visualization of time-varying weather ensembles across multiple resolutions. *IEEE transactions on visualization and computer graphics*, 23(1):841–850.

John Burkardt. Accessed: 2025-01-30. John burkardt's homepage. `https://people.sc.fsu.edu/~jburkardt/`.

Le Chen, Bin Lei, Dunzhi Zhou, Pei-Hung Lin, Chunhua Liao, Caiwen Ding, and Ali Jannesari. 2024. Fortran2cpp: Automating fortran-to-c++ migration using llms via multi-turn dialogue and dual-agent integration. *Preprint*, arXiv:2412.19770.

Yen-Chi Chen. 2017. A tutorial on kernel density estimation and recent advances. *Biostatistics & Epidemiology*, 1(1):161–187.

Michel Cuer and Roger Bayer. 1980. Fortran routines for linear inverse problems. *Geophysics*, 45(11):1706–1719.

Marie de Groot. 2024. Are those 700,000 large language models (llms) on hugging face really necessary? Medium, published June 28, 2024; accessed January 30, 2025.

Joseph M Derlaga, Tyrone Phillips, and Christopher J Roy. 2013. Sensei computational fluid dynamics code: a case study in modern fortran software development. In *21st AIAA Computational Fluid Dynamics Conference*, page 2450.

Murali Emani, Zhen Xie, Siddhisanket Raskar, Varuni Sastry, William Arnold, Bruce Wilson, Rajeev Thakur, Venkatram Vishwanath, Zhengchun Liu, Michael E. Papka, Cindy Orozco Bohorquez, Rick Weisner, Karen Li, Yongning Sheng, Yun Du, Jian Zhang, Alexander Tsyplikhin, Gurdaman Khaira, Jeremy Fowers, Ramakrishnan Sivakumar, Victoria Godsoe, Adrian Macias, Chetan Tekur, and Matthew Boyd. 2022. A comprehensive evaluation of novel ai accelerators for deep learning workloads. In *2022 IEEE/ACM International Workshop on Performance Modeling, Benchmarking and Simulation of High Performance Computer Systems (PMBS)*, pages 13–25.

Stuart I Feldman. 1990. A fortran to c converter. In *ACM SIGPLAN Fortran Forum*, volume 9, pages 21–22. ACM New York, NY, USA.

Artur Gramacki. 2018. *Nonparametric kernel density estimation and its computational aspects*, volume 37. Springer.

Ralf W Grosse-Kunstleve, Nicholas K Sauter, Nigel W Moriarty, and Paul D Adams. 2002. The computational crystallography toolbox: crystallographic algorithms in a reusable software framework. *Applied Crystallography*, 35(1):126–136.

Ralf W Grosse-Kunstleve, Thomas C Terwilliger, Nicholas K Sauter, and Paul D Adams. 2012. Automatic fortran to c++ conversion with fable. *Source code for biology and medicine*, 7:1–11.

Jordan Hoffmann, Sebastian Borgeaud, Arthur Mensch, Elena Buchatskaya, Trevor Cai, Eliza Rutherford, Diego de Las Casas, Lisa Anne Hendricks, Johannes Welbl, Aidan Clark, Tom Hennigan, Eric Noland, Katie Millican, George van den Driessche, Bogdan Damoc, Aurelia Guy, Simon Osindero, Karen Simonyan, Erich Elsen, Oriol Vinyals, Jack W. Rae, and Laurent Sifre. 2022. Training compute-optimal large language models. In *Proceedings of the 36th International Conference on Neural Information Processing Systems*, NIPS '22, Red Hook, NY, USA. Curran Associates Inc.

Matthew A Jaro. 1989. Advances in record-linkage methodology as applied to matching the 1985 census of tampa, florida. *Journal of the American Statistical Association*, 84(406):414–420.

Wenxiang Jiao, Wenxuan Wang, Jen-Tse Huang, Xing Wang, and Zhaopeng Tu. 2023. Is chatgpt a good translator? yes with gpt-4 as the engine.

Benjamin Knobloch, Christine Sweeney, Ayan Biswas, and Shawn M. Jones. 2025. Metadata tracking and analysis of llm-based source-to-source code translation. In *Proceedings of the 2025 Conference on Data Analysis*.

Dimitri Komatitsch and Jeroen Tromp. 2002. Spectral-element simulations of global seismic wave propagation—i. validation. *Geophysical Journal International*, 149(2):390–412.

Woosuk Kwon, Zhuohan Li, Siyuan Zhuang, Ying Sheng, Lianmin Zheng, Cody Hao Yu, Joseph E. Gonzalez, Hao Zhang, and Ion Stoica. 2023. Efficient memory management for large language model serving with pagedattention. In *Proceedings of the ACM SIGOPS 29th Symposium on Operating Systems Principles*.

Bin Lei, Caiwen Ding, Le Chen, Pei-Hung Lin, and Chunhua Liao. 2023. Creating a dataset for high-performance computing code translation using llms: A bridge between openmp fortran and c++. In *2023 IEEE High Performance Extreme Computing Conference (HPEC)*, pages 1–7. IEEE.

Chunhua Liao, Pei-Hung Lin, Joshua Asplund, Markus Schordan, and Ian Karlin. 2017. Dataracebench: a benchmark suite for systematic evaluation of data race detection tools. In *Proceedings of the International Conference for High Performance Computing, Networking, Storage and Analysis*, SC '17, New York, NY, USA. Association for Computing Machinery.

Pengfei Liu, Weizhe Yuan, Jinlan Fu, Zhengbao Jiang, Hiroaki Hayashi, and Graham Neubig. 2023. Pre-train, prompt, and predict: A systematic survey of prompting methods in natural language processing. *ACM computing surveys*, 55(9):1–35.

Richard Tran Mills, Chuan Lu, Peter C Lichtner, and Glenn E Hammond. 2007. Simulating subsurface flow and transport on ultrascale computers using pflotran. In *Journal of physics: conference series*, volume 78, page 012051. IOP Publishing.

David R Musser and Atul Saini. 1995. *The STL Tutorial and Reference Guide: C++ Programming with the Standard Template Library*. Addison Wesley Longman Publishing Co., Inc.

Mariano Méndez, Fernando G. Tinetti, and Jeffrey L. Overbey. 2014. Climate models: Challenges for fortran development tools. In *2014 Second International Workshop on Software Engineering for High Performance Computing in Computational Science and Engineering*, pages 6–12.

M Nardelli. 1995. Parst95–an update to parst: a system of fortran routines for calculating molecular structure parameters from the results of crystal structure analyses. *Applied Crystallography*, 28(5):659–659.

Cesar Ocampo and Juan Senent. 2006. The design and development of copernicus: A comprehensive trajectory design and optimization system. In *57th International Astronautical Congress*, pages C1–4.

Rangeet Pan, Ali Reza Ibrahimzada, Rahul Krishna, Divya Sankar, Lambert Pouguem Wassi, Michele Merler, Boris Sobolev, Raju Pavuluri, Saurabh Sinha, and Reyhaneh Jabbarvand. 2024. Lost in translation: A study of bugs introduced by large language models while translating code. In *Proceedings of the IEEE/ACM 46th International Conference on Software Engineering*, ICSE '24, New York, NY, USA. Association for Computing Machinery.

Rocco Pietrini, Marina Paolanti, and Emanuele Frontoni. 2024. Bridging eras: Transforming fortran legacies into python with the power of large language models. In *2024 IEEE 3rd International Conference on Computing and Machine Intelligence (ICMI)*, pages 1–5. IEEE.

Raghu Prabhakar, Ram Sivaramakrishnan, Darshan Gandhi, Yun Du, Mingran Wang, Xiangyu Song, Kejie Zhang, Tianren Gao, Angela Wang, Xiaoyan Li, Yongning Sheng, Joshua Brot, Denis Sokolov, Apurv Vivek, Calvin Leung, Arjun Sabnis, Jiayu Bai, Tuowen Zhao, Mark Gottscho, David Jackson, Mark Luttrell, Manish K. Shah, Zhengyu Chen, Kaizhao Liang, Swayambhoo Jain, Urmish Thakker, Dawei Huang, Sumti Jairath, Kevin J. Brown, and Kunle Olukotun. 2024. Sambanova sn40l: Scaling the ai memory wall with dataflow and composition of experts. In *2024 57th IEEE/ACM International Symposium on Microarchitecture (MICRO)*, page 1353–1366. IEEE.

Shuo Ren, Daya Guo, Shuai Lu, Long Zhou, Shujie Liu, Duyu Tang, Neel Sundaresan, Ming Zhou, Ambrosio Blanco, and Shuai Ma. 2020. Codebleu: a method for automatic evaluation of code synthesis. *arXiv preprint arXiv:2009.10297*.

Rosetta Code Community. 2025. Rosetta code: Programming chrestomathy site. Accessed: 2025-03-03.

SambaNova. Sambanova cloud. Accessed: March 8, 2025.

Galen M Shipman and Timothy C Randles. 2023. An evaluation of risks associated with relying on fortran for mission critical codes for the next 15 years. Technical report, Los Alamos National Laboratory (LANL), Los Alamos, NM, United States.

B. W. Silverman. 1998. *Density Estimation for Statistics and Data Analysis*, 1st ed. edition. Routledge.

G. Theurich, B. Anson, N.A. Hill, and A. Hill. 2001. Making the fortran-to-c transition: how painful is it really? *Computing in Science Engineering*, 3(1):21–27.

Hugo Touvron, Thibaut Lavril, Gautier Izacard, Xavier Martinet, Marie-Anne Lachaux, Timothée Lacroix, Baptiste Rozière, Naman Goyal, Eric Hambro, Faisal Azhar, Aurelien Rodriguez, Armand Joulin, Edouard Grave, and Guillaume Lample. 2023. Llama: Open and efficient foundation language models. *Preprint*, arXiv:2302.13971.

Todd L Veldhuizen and M Ed Jernigan. 1997. Will c++ be faster than fortran? In *International Conference on Computing in Object-Oriented Parallel Environments*, pages 49–56. Springer.

Jianxun Wang and Yixiang Chen. 2023. A review on code generation with llms: Application and evaluation. In *2023 IEEE International Conference on Medical Artificial Intelligence (MedAI)*, pages 284–289.

Laurie S Waters, Gregg W McKinney, Joe W Durkee, Michael L Fensin, John S Hendricks, Michael R James, Russell C Johns, and Denise B Pelowitz. 2007. The mcnpx monte carlo radiation transport code. In *AIP conference Proceedings*, volume 896, pages 81–90. American Institute of Physics.

Yuanbo Wen, Qi Guo, Qiang Fu, Xiaqing Li, Jianxing Xu, Yanlin Tang, Yongwei Zhao, Xin Hu, Zidong Du, Ling Li, Chao Wang, Xuehai Zhou, and Yunji Chen. 2022a. Babeltower: Learning to auto-parallelized program translation. In *International Conference on Machine Learning*.

Yuanbo Wen, Qi Guo, Qiang Fu, Xiaqing Li, Jianxing Xu, Yanlin Tang, Yongwei Zhao, Xing Hu, Zidong Du, Ling Li, Chao Wang, Xuehai Zhou, and Yunji Chen. 2022b. BabelTower: Learning to auto-parallelized program translation. In *Proceedings of the 39th International Conference on Machine Learning*, volume 162 of *Proceedings of Machine Learning Research*, pages 23685–23700. PMLR.

William .E. Winkler. 1990. String comparator metrics and enhanced decision rules in the fellegi-sunter model of record linkage. Available online.

Weixiang Yan, Yuchen Tian, Yunzhe Li, Qian Chen, and Wen Wang. 2023. Codetransocean: A comprehensive multilingual benchmark for code translation. *arXiv preprint arXiv:2310.04951*.

Tianyu Zheng, Ge Zhang, Tianhao Shen, Xueling Liu, Bill Yuchen Lin, Jie Fu, Wenhu Chen, and Xiang Yue. 2025. Opencodeinterpreter: Integrating code generation with execution and refinement. *Preprint*, arXiv:2402.14658.

FlavorDiffusion: Modeling Food-Chemical Interactions with Diffusion

Joomidang AI Research

Junpyo Seo* Dongwan Kim*

jpseo99@joomidang.com ryankim@joomidang.com

Jaewook Jeong Inkyu Park Junho Min

jwjeong@joomidang.com s52091851@joomidang.com minjh0113@joomidang.com

Abstract

The study of food pairing has evolved beyond subjective expertise with the advent of machine learning. This paper presents FlavorDiffusion, a novel framework leveraging diffusion models to predict food-chemical interactions and ingredient pairings without relying on chromatography. By integrating graph-based embeddings [Perozzi et al., 2014], diffusion processes [Ho et al., 2020, Song et al., 2021, Sun and Yang, 2023], and chemical property encoding [Azambuja et al., 2023], FlavorDiffusion addresses data imbalances and enhances clustering quality. Using a heterogeneous graph derived from datasets like Recipe1M [Marín et al., 2019] and FlavorDB, our model demonstrates superior performance in reconstructing ingredient-ingredient relationships. The addition of a Chemical Structure Prediction (CSP) layer further refines the embedding space, achieving state-of-the-art NMI scores and enabling meaningful discovery of novel ingredient combinations. The proposed framework represents a significant step forward in computational gastronomy, offering scalable, interpretable, and chemically informed solutions for food science. The source code and dataset used in this study are publicly available at https://github.com/Giventicket/FlavorDiffusion.

1 Introduction

Food pairing has traditionally relied on the intuition and experience of chefs, yet scientific analysis and optimization of food combinations remain underexplored. Recent research has leveraged data-driven approaches to model the relationships between food ingredients and chemical compounds to predict novel food pairings.

Several computational approaches have been developed to model food pairings and ingredient relationships. Kitchenette [Park et al., 2021], for instance, applies Siamese neural networks to predict and recommend ingredient pairings based on a large annotated dataset. However, it suffers from key limitations, such as a lack of chemical interpretability and heavy reliance on labeled data, making it less generalizable across different cuisines and novel food combinations.

One of the key advancements in this domain is FlavorGraph [Park et al., 2021], a large-scale food-chemical deep neural network model comprising 6,653 ingredient nodes and 1,645 compound nodes. This graph captures two primary relationships: (1) ingredient-ingredient relations, representing co-occurrence patterns in recipes, and (2) ingredient-compound relations, indicating chemical composition links. These relationships are constructed using datasets such as Recipe1M [Marín et al., 2019], FlavorDB, and HyperFoods. FlavorGraph incorporates food-chemical associations into a neural network by leveraging the metapath2vec [Dong et al., 2017] algorithm, which embeds ingredient-compound relationships in a word2vec-like manner. Expanding on this approach, WineGraph [Gawrysiak et al., 2023] extends the framework by integrating wine-related datasets to define optimal food-wine pairings.

Despite progress in computational food science, major challenges remain. Chromatography-based methods, while precise, are costly and limit the acquisition of large-scale chemical interaction data. FlavorGraph effectively captures ingredient-compound relationships using metapath-based embeddings, but its reliance on random-walk sampling makes it difficult to incorporate edge weights and spatial information within the graph structure. These limitations hinder the full exploitation of food-chemical associations, leading to suboptimal ingredient relationship modeling. To address these challenges, we introduce FlavorDiffusion, a Diffusion Model-based framework that refines the representation of food-chemical interactions and ele-

*Co-first authors.

Proceedings of the 1st Workshop on AI and Scientific Discovery: Directions and Opportunities, pages 70–77
May 3, 2025 ©2025 Association for Computational Linguistics

vates the quality of food pairing predictions.

Contributions

- We propose a graph-based diffusion modeling approach that leverages DIFUSCO [Sun and Yang, 2023] to capture richer and more structured representations of food-chemical interactions.

- We introduce a balanced subgraph sampling strategy to address data imbalance issues, ensuring fair representation across different ingredient-chemical associations.

- Our experimental results demonstrate improvements in Normalized Pointwise Mutual Information (NPMI) scores for node embeddings, facilitating more effective chemical inference.

- We establish a foundation for predicting chromatography results for non-hub chemicals, extending the applicability of our model beyond frequently occurring compounds.

- Our approach enables pairing inference using chemical properties, providing structured and interpretable recommendations for novel ingredient combinations.

2 Dataset

Our study builds upon FlavorGraph [Park et al., 2021] by utilizing the same large-scale datasets to construct a robust food-chemical network. These datasets provide a structured representation of ingredient relationships and chemical interactions. In the following sections, we summarize the key characteristics of these datasets and outline the preprocessing steps applied to ensure data consistency and usability in our framework.

Type	Source	Nodes	Edges
I-I	Recipe1M	6,653	111,355
I-FC	FlavorDB	1,561	35,440
I-DC	HyperFoods	84	386
Total	-	8,298	147,181

Table 1: Summary of the heterogeneous food-compound graph. I-I represents ingredient ingredient co-occurrence from Recipe1M, I-FC denotes ingredient-flavor compound associations from FlavorDB, and I-DC refers to ingredient-drug compound relations

2.1 Data Sources

This study utilizes the same datasets as FlavorGraph [Park et al., 2021] to construct a structured food-chemical network.

Recipe1M [Marín et al., 2019] contains 65,284 recipes with ingredient lists and cooking instructions, capturing ingredient co-occurrence patterns in real-world culinary practices.

FlavorDB compiles chemical composition data from multiple sources, including *FooDB*, *Flavornet*, and *BitterDB*. It originally includes 2,254 flavor compounds linked to 936 food ingredients, but only 400 commonly used ingredients were selected to align with Recipe1M, resulting in 1,561 flavor compound nodes and 164,531 ingredient-flavor compound edges.

HyperFoods maps drug compounds to food ingredients using machine learning based on food-gene interactions. From the original 206 food ingredients, 104 were selected, yielding 84 drug compound nodes and 386 ingredient-drug compound edges.

2.2 Data Processing

To construct a structured representation of food-chemical relationships, we build upon FlavorGraph [Park et al., 2021], a heterogeneous graph that integrates both culinary and chemical associations. The graph construction process follows a structured approach. First, an ingredient-ingredient graph is built by extracting co-occurrence patterns from Recipe1M [Marín et al., 2019], where edges between ingredients are established based on their Normalized Pointwise Mutual Information (NPMI) scores. Only statistically significant ingredient pairs appearing together in a substantial number of recipes are retained, resulting in a total of 111,355 edges. Second, an ingredient-chemical graph is formed by linking ingredients to their corresponding chemical compounds using FlavorDB and HyperFoods, leading to 35,440 edges between food ingredients and known chemical compounds. The final graph structure comprises 6,653 ingredient nodes and 1,645 compound nodes, forming a heterogeneous graph that encodes both culinary co-occurrence relationships and chemical interactions.

2.3 Chemical Property Encoding

To ensure chemically informed ingredient representations, each compound is characterized using CACTVS chemical fingerprints, which are encoded as 881-dimensional binary vectors. These vectors represent molecular descriptors such as molecular weight, functional groups, and substructure patterns, using a binary encoding scheme where each bit indicates the presence or absence of a specific chemical substructure.

3 Related Work

3.1 FlavorGraph

FlavorGraph [Park et al., 2021] is a heterogeneous graph $G = (V, E)$ integrating ingredient co-occurrence and molecular profiling to model food-chemical interactions. By leveraging metapath-based learning [Dong et al., 2017], it enables systematic ingredient discovery and predictive food pairing through shared molecular properties.

3.1.1 Metapath2Vec

To learn chemically meaningful embeddings, we employ **Metapath2Vec**, which captures high-order relations via structured random walks. Ingredients are classified into hub ingredients (H), which directly connect to chemical compounds, and non-hub ingredients (N), which lack direct chemical links and rely on hub ingredients to acquire chemical insights.

The metapath sampling strategy follows:

$$N \rightarrow H \rightarrow C \rightarrow H \rightarrow N$$

where C represents chemical compounds. This structured propagation ensures that non-hub ingredients inherit chemical relevance, enhancing embedding robustness and interpretability.

3.1.2 Architecture

The network, parameterized by θ, takes node pairs (i, j) as input and outputs an edge score $s_\theta(i, j)$, normalized across all embeddings:

$$s_\theta(i, j) = \sigma(\mathbf{u}_i^T \mathbf{u}_j)$$

where $\mathbf{u}_i$ and $\mathbf{u}_j$ are the learned embeddings for nodes i and j, ensuring consistency across culinary co-occurrence and chemical similarity.

3.1.3 Loss Function

Embeddings are optimized using Skip-Gram with Negative Sampling (SGNS):

$$J_\theta = \sum_{(i,j)\in D} \log \sigma(\mathbf{u}_i^T \mathbf{u}_j) + \sum_{(i,j')\in D'} \log \sigma(-\mathbf{u}_i^T \mathbf{u}_{j'})$$

where D and D' are positive and negative sample pairs. To enforce chemical relevance, an additional **Chemical Structure Prediction (CSP)** loss is introduced:

$$L_{\text{CSP},\theta} = \sum_{d=1}^{D} [y_d \log f_{\theta,d}(i) + (1 - y_d) \log (1 - f_{\theta,d}(i))]$$

where $f_{\theta,d}(i)$ predicts the presence of the d-th molecular substructure y_d, refining embeddings with molecular fingerprints.

3.2 DIFUSCO

Graph-based diffusion models have proven effective for combinatorial optimization. We apply the Gaussian diffusion framework to reconstruct structured graphs, enhancing the predictive accuracy of food-chemical interactions while preserving interpretability. By integrating diffusion-driven embeddings into a heterogeneous network, our approach seamlessly incorporates molecular insights into ingredient pairing research, advancing computational gastronomy.

4 Proposition: FlavorDiffusion

4.1 Sub-Graph Sampling

FlavorDiffusion is built upon the DIFUSCO Gaussian noise-based diffusion model, extending its capabilities to structured food-chemical graphs. The core objective is to train a model capable of reconstructing subgraphs sampled from the full heterogeneous graph $G = (V, E)$ while leveraging node attributes as guidance.

The full graph consists of a diverse set of nodes V, including hub ingredients, non-hub ingredients, flavor compounds, and drug compounds, with edges E encoding the strength of their relationships as continuous values in $[0, 1]$. We define a dataset of subgraphs, where each sample contains m nodes selected from G. These subgraphs are denoted as:

$$\mathcal{D}_m = \{G_i = (V_i, E_i)\}_{i=1}^{N},$$

where each subgraph G_i has $|V_i| = m$ nodes and an adjacency matrix E_i of size $m \times m$, representing pairwise edge scores. The dataset is partitioned into training (N_t) and validation (N_v) subsets.

4.2 Forward Diffusion Process

For a single data point $G_i = (V_i, E_i)$ sampled from the dataset, we define the diffusion process over its edge set E_i. By convention, we denote the corrupted version of E_i at timestep t as x_t, aligning with standard diffusion formalisms. The node representations, encompassing all vertex features, are denoted as $\mathbf{Emb}$.

The forward diffusion process follows a Markovian Gaussian noise injection, progressively perturbing the edges x_t while preserving node representations:

$$q(x_t|x_{t-1}) = \mathcal{N}(x_t; \sqrt{1-\beta_t}x_{t-1}, \beta_t I),$$

where β_t is a predefined noise variance at timestep t. Given an initial clean edge matrix $x_0 = E_i$, we can analytically express the direct corruption of x_0 at any timestep t as:

$$q(x_t|x_0) = \mathcal{N}(x_t; \sqrt{\bar{\alpha}_t}x_0, (1-\bar{\alpha}_t)I),$$

where $\bar{\alpha}_t = \prod_{s=1}^{t}(1-\beta_s)$ represents the cumulative noise effect over time. This formulation allows direct sampling of x_t from x_0, bypassing iterative updates.

In this framework, the edge structure is progressively degraded into Gaussian noise, while node representations $\mathbf{Emb}$ remain unchanged, ensuring that denoising relies on learned node attributes.

4.3 Reverse Denoising Process

The reverse process seeks to recover x_0 from the fully corrupted state x_T, learning to remove noise in a stepwise manner. The key assumption is that the forward process follows a Gaussian transition, enabling an analytically derived reverse process.

Given the Markovian nature of the diffusion process, we define the true posterior:

$$q(x_{t-1}|x_t, x_0) = \mathcal{N}(x_{t-1}; \tilde{\mu}_t(x_t, x_0), \tilde{\beta}_t I),$$

where the posterior mean and variance are derived as:

$$\tilde{\mu}_t(x_t, x_0) = \frac{\sqrt{\bar{\alpha}_{t-1}}\beta_t}{1-\bar{\alpha}_t}x_0 + \frac{\sqrt{\alpha_t}(1-\bar{\alpha}_{t-1})}{1-\bar{\alpha}_t}x_t,$$

$$\tilde{\beta}_t = \frac{1-\bar{\alpha}_{t-1}}{1-\bar{\alpha}_t}\beta_t.$$

Since x_0 is unknown, we train a model $p_\theta(x_0|x_t)$ to approximate it. Substituting the predicted x_0, the learned reverse process is modeled as:

$$p_\theta(x_{t-1}|x_t, \mathbf{Emb}) = \mathcal{N}\big(x_{t-1}; \mu_\theta(x_t, t, \mathbf{Emb}), \Sigma_\theta(x_t, t)\big),$$

where μ_θ is the learned estimate for $\tilde{\mu}_t(x_t, x_0)$, and the variance term is fixed as $\Sigma_\theta(x_t, t) = \tilde{\beta}_t I$, avoiding the need for explicit learning. The function μ_θ is now conditioned on the node representations ($\mathbf{Emb}$) of the two vertices forming the edge.

Using the DDPM convention, we parameterize μ_θ as:

$$\mu_\theta(x_t, t, \mathbf{Emb}) = \frac{1}{\sqrt{\alpha_t}}\left(x_t - \frac{\beta_t}{\sqrt{1-\bar{\alpha}_t}}\epsilon_\theta(x_t, t, \mathbf{Emb})\right),$$

where $\epsilon_\theta(x_t, t, \mathbf{Emb})$ is the learned noise estimate, which is now explicitly conditioned on the representations of the two nodes forming the edge. The node representations provide additional context for denoising by leveraging node-specific features.

4.4 Optimization via Variational Lower Bound

To train the reverse model, we maximize the variational lower bound (ELBO), decomposed as:

$$\mathcal{L}_{\text{ELBO}} = E_q\Bigg[\log p_\theta(x_0|x_1, \mathbf{Emb}) - \sum_{t=1}^{T} D_{\text{KL}}\big(q(x_{t-1}|x_t, x_0)\|p_\theta(x_{t-1}|x_t, \mathbf{Emb})\big)\Bigg].$$

Here, T represents the total number of diffusion steps, defining the depth of the forward and reverse process. The KL divergence encourages the learned transitions to match the true posterior. Since $q(x_t|x_0)$ is Gaussian, minimizing D_{KL} is equivalent to predicting the noise component ϵ added during diffusion. Thus, the training objective simplifies to:

$$\mathcal{L}_{\text{recon}} = E_{t,x_0,\epsilon}\left[\|\epsilon - \epsilon_\theta(x_t, t, \mathbf{Emb})\|^2\right].$$

This loss ensures that ϵ_θ effectively estimates the noise introduced in the forward process while incorporating node representations. By iteratively refining the denoising function, FlavorDiffusion reconstructs the original ingredient-ingredient graph from noisy subgraphs, leveraging both the structural edge information and node attributes to enhance predictive modeling for food pairing analysis.

4.5 Inference

Graph reconstruction follows Denoising Diffusion Implicit Models (DDIM) for efficient and deterministic sampling. Unlike DDPM, DDIM removes noise via a non-Markovian update, accelerating inference.

Starting from $x_T \sim \mathcal{N}(0, I)$, the reverse process iterates:

$$x_{t-1} = \sqrt{\bar{\alpha}_{t-1}}\hat{x}_0 + \sqrt{1 - \bar{\alpha}_{t-1}} \cdot \epsilon_\theta(x_t, t, \mathbf{Emb}),$$

where the predicted clean graph is:

$$\hat{x}_0 = \frac{x_t - \sqrt{1 - \bar{\alpha}_t}\epsilon_\theta(x_t, t, \mathbf{Emb})}{\sqrt{\bar{\alpha}_t}}.$$

Iterating from T to 0, the model refines x_t to recover ingredient-ingredient relationships. DDIM ensures fast, stable, and chemically meaningful reconstructions.

4.6 Model Architecture

The noise prediction network $\epsilon_\theta(x_t, t, \mathbf{V})$ employs an anisotropic GNN to iteratively refine node and edge embeddings. Let $h_i^\ell \in \mathbf{R}^d$ and $e_{ij}^\ell \in \mathbf{R}^{d_e}$ denote the node and edge features at layer ℓ, respectively. The refinement process updates both edge and node embeddings through the following operations:

Edge Refinement The initial edge embeddings e_{ij}^0 are set as the corresponding values from the noisy edge representation x_t. At each layer ℓ, the intermediate edge embeddings $\hat{e}_{ij}^\ell$ are updated as:

$$\hat{e}_{ij}^\ell = P^\ell e_{ij}^\ell + Q^\ell h_i^\ell + R^\ell h_j^\ell,$$

where $P^\ell, Q^\ell, R^\ell \in \mathbf{R}^{d_e \times d_e}$ are learnable parameters. The refined edge embedding $e_{ij}^{\ell+1}$ is then computed as:

$$e_{ij}^{\ell+1} = e_{ij}^\ell + \text{MLP}_e\big(\text{BN}(\hat{e}_{ij}^\ell)\big) + \text{MLP}_t(t),$$

where MLP_e is a 2-layer perceptron and MLP_t embeds the diffusion timestep t using sinusoidal features.

Node Refinement The node embeddings h_i^ℓ are refined by aggregating information from neighboring nodes and their associated edges. The update rule for $h_i^{\ell+1}$ is given by:

$$h_i^{\ell+1} = h_i^\ell + \alpha \cdot \text{BN}\Big(U^\ell h_i^\ell + \sum_{j \in \mathcal{N}(i)} \sigma(\hat{e}_{ij}^\ell) \odot V^\ell h_j^\ell\Big),$$

where $U^\ell, V^\ell \in \mathbf{R}^{d \times d}$ are learnable parameter matrices, σ is the sigmoid activation function used for edge gating, $\odot$ denotes the Hadamard (element-wise) product, $\mathcal{N}(i)$ represents the set of neighbors for node i, and α is the ReLU activation applied after aggregation.

Final Prediction After L GNN layers, the final refined edge embeddings $E^{(L)} \in \mathbf{R}^{N \times N \times d_e}$ are passed through a ReLU activation and a multi-layer perceptron (MLP) to predict the noise:

$$\epsilon_\theta(x_t, t, \mathbf{V}) = \text{MLP}\big(\text{ReLU}(E^{(L)})\big).$$

This formulation ensures that both node and edge embeddings are iteratively refined to capture local and global graph structure, enabling robust denoising and reconstruction of ingredient-ingredient relationships.

5 Experimental Results

The evaluation consists of two primary experiments: (1) reproducing the NMI-based clustering performance evaluation originally conducted in FlavorGraph, and (2) assessing the generalization ability of our proposed Flavor Diffusion framework by testing on subgraphs of different sizes.

Subgraphs of size 25, 50, 100, and 200 nodes were sampled while maintaining an equal proportion of hub and non-hub ingredients. The number of subgraphs used for training and testing at each scale is shown in Table 2.

Table 2: Subgraph Composition for Training and Testing

Nodes per Subgraph	Train Set Size	Test Set Size
25	256,000	256
50	128,000	128
100	64,000	64
200	32,000	32

Generalization Ability To assess the generalization ability of the proposed framework, models trained on one subgraph size were tested on all sizes to observe performance across different scales. The results in Table 3 indicate that models trained on 25-node subgraphs generalize poorly to larger graphs, with an MSE of 0.025078 when tested on 100-node subgraphs. In contrast, the 100-node trained model demonstrates the most stable generalization across different test sizes, showing minimal MSE variation. The 200-node trained model, while excelling on large graphs with an MSE of 0.003692, exhibits difficulties in adapting to smaller structures, with a high error of 0.059557 when tested on 25-node subgraphs.

Table 3: Generalization Performance: Validation MSE Loss

Train Size	Test (25)	Test (50)	Test (100)	Test (200)
25	0.004589	0.010965	0.025078	0.019477
50	0.025235	0.005884	0.004420	0.004123
100	**0.003964**	**0.003678**	0.004232	0.003953
200	0.059557	0.007837	**0.003992**	**0.003692**

These results highlight that subgraph size significantly impacts both intra-subgraph clustering and cross-subgraph generalization performance. The Flavor Diffusion (100 nodes) model provides the best balance between clustering accuracy and scalability, demonstrating the ability to generalize well across varying ingredient graph structures. On the other hand, training on extremely small subgraphs limits generalization, while models trained on large subgraphs struggle when applied to smaller ingredient sets. These findings suggest that a mid-sized subgraph training approach (e.g., 100 nodes) is optimal for robust ingredient representation learning.

NMI-based Evaluation To construct the clustering test dataset, nine representative food categories were defined: *Bakery/Dessert/Snack, Beverage Alcoholic, Cereal/Crop/Bean, Dairy, Fruit, Meat/Animal Product, Plant/Vegetable, Seafood, and Others*. From these, 416 chemical hub ingredients with strong connections were selected to ensure diverse and well-defined clustering labels, enabling fair comparisons across models commonly used in related studies.

The NMI-based evaluation results in Table 4 demonstrate the clustering quality of different models. Among the non-CSP variants, the Flavor Diffusion (50 nodes) model achieves the highest NMI score of 0.3236, surpassing the baseline FlavorGraph model without CSP. The best overall performance is observed in the Flavor Diffusion_CSP (200 nodes) model, which achieves an NMI score of 0.3410, indicating that the CSP layer significantly improves the learned ingredient embeddings. Smaller subgraphs, such as the 25-node configuration, show the greatest improvement when using CSP (0.2970 vs. 0.2167), suggesting that the chemical structure prediction enhances clustering, particularly in more limited ingredient sets.

Table 4: Performance Comparison Using NMI Metric. *CSP shorts for chemical structure prediction.

Model	NMI Mean	NMI Std
FlavorGraph [Park et al., 2021]	0.2995	0.0403
FlavorGraph_CSP [Park et al., 2021]	0.3102	0.0407
Flavor Diffusion (25 nodes)	0.2167	0.0319
Flavor Diffusion (50 nodes)	**0.3236**	**0.0134**
Flavor Diffusion (100 nodes)	0.3170	0.0207
Flavor Diffusion (200 nodes)	0.2935	0.0300
Flavor Diffusion_CSP (25 nodes)	0.2970	0.0144
Flavor Diffusion_CSP (50 nodes)	0.2862	0.0152
Flavor Diffusion_CSP (100 nodes)	0.3169	0.0257
Flavor Diffusion_CSP (200 nodes)	**0.3410**	**0.0150**

6 Discussion

The visualization results highlight the impact of the proposed Flavor Diffusion framework on embedding quality, particularly with the CSP (Chemical Structure Prediction) layer, as shown in Figures 1 and 2.

Dynamic Reconstruction for Novel Insights The iterative reconstruction process visualized in Figure 1 showcases the Flavor Diffusion framework's ability to refine ingredient-ingredient relationships progressively. Starting from random initialization (Step 0), the edge scores evolve over diffusion steps, ultimately converging towards the ground truth structure by Step 10. The color intensity of the edges reflects their normalized scores, with higher values indicating stronger relationships. This gradual alignment with the ground truth demonstrates the model's capacity to encode meaningful relational patterns in a structured manner.

Embedding Space Analysis Figure 2 compares embedding spaces across model configurations. The baseline embeddings (left) show poor separation, forming diffuse clusters dominated by non-hub ingredients.

Flavor Diffusion (200 nodes) without CSP (center) improves clustering by grouping chemical compounds and hub ingredients, though some overlap

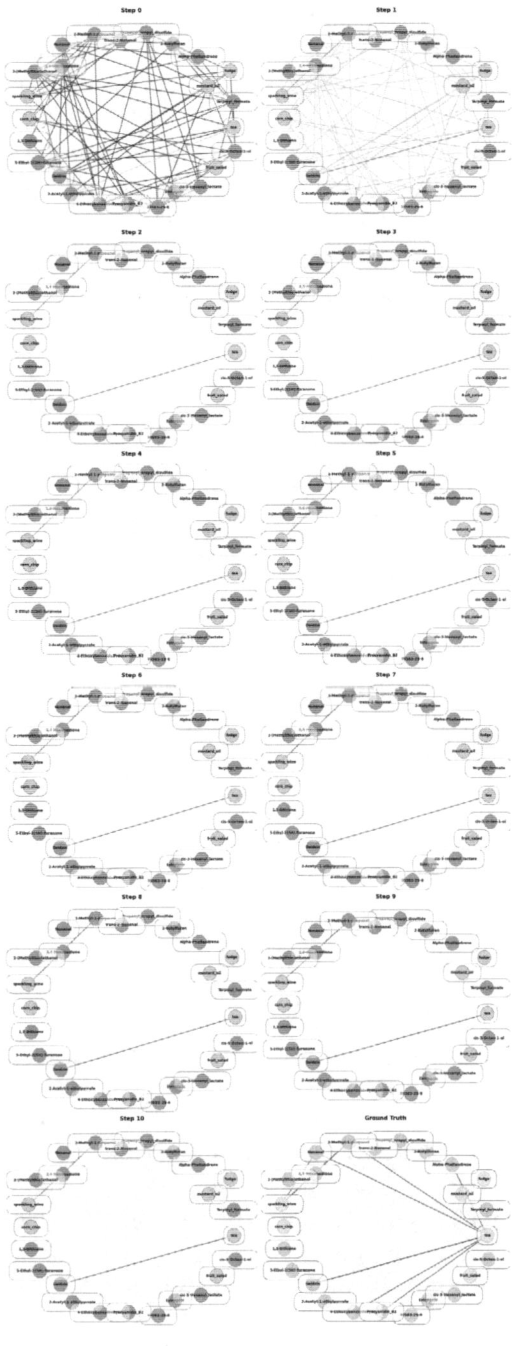

Figure 1: Progression of edge scores over diffusion steps for a 25-node subgraph. The color intensity represents edge scores normalized between 0 and 1. The reconstructed graph increasingly aligns with the ground truth structure.

remains. Adding the CSP layer (right) further refines the structure, yielding anisotropic clusters that better capture ingredient-compound relationships.

Potential for Ingredient Innovation To evaluate the predictive capacity of Flavor Diffusion, we randomly sampled 100 nodes and computed the mean edge score over 100,000 inferred edges. This large-scale evaluation ensures that the model captures both established and novel ingredient relationships, supporting its ability to reconstruct known pairings while suggesting unexplored flavor synergies.

Table 5: Top 5 High-Confidence Ingredient Pairings

Ingredient 1	Ingredient 2	Mean Score	Std Dev
Red Chili Powder	Turmeric Powder	0.7114	0.0882
Coriander Powder	Turmeric Powder	0.6057	0.0827
Asafoetida Powder	Turmeric Powder	0.5930	0.0846
Garam Masala Powder	Turmeric Powder	0.5178	0.1055
Cumin Powder	Turmeric Powder	0.4663	0.1525

These pairings align with traditional spice blends, frequently observed in Indian and Southeast Asian cuisine. Their strong co-occurrence validates Flavor Diffusion's ability to model established ingredient relationships. Beyond known pairings, the model also proposes conceptually novel combinations, potentially inspiring new culinary applications.

Table 6: Top 5 Creative Ingredient Pairings Suggested by Flavor Diffusion

Ingredient 1	Ingredient 2	Mean Score	Std Dev
Soy Sauce	Vanilla Extract	0.0006	0.0001
Garlic Paste	Dark Chocolate	0.0005	0.0001
Cumin Powder	Coffee Beans	0.0004	0.0002
Green Cardamom	Parmesan Cheese	0.0003	0.0002
Olive Oil	Black Tea	0.0004	0.0001

These unconventional combinations introduce potential for umami-sweet fusion (Soy Sauce, Vanilla Extract), savory-bitter contrast (Garlic Paste, Dark Chocolate), and aromatic synergies (Cumin Powder, Coffee Beans and Green Cardamom, Parmesan Cheese). Such findings demonstrate that Flavor Diffusion extends beyond known ingredient interactions, offering a data-driven approach for novel flavor discovery and AI-assisted recipe development.

Alignment with Culinary and Chemical Properties The reconstructed graphs closely align with ground truth structures, demonstrating the model's fidelity in capturing both culinary and chemical relationships. As diffusion progresses, the model

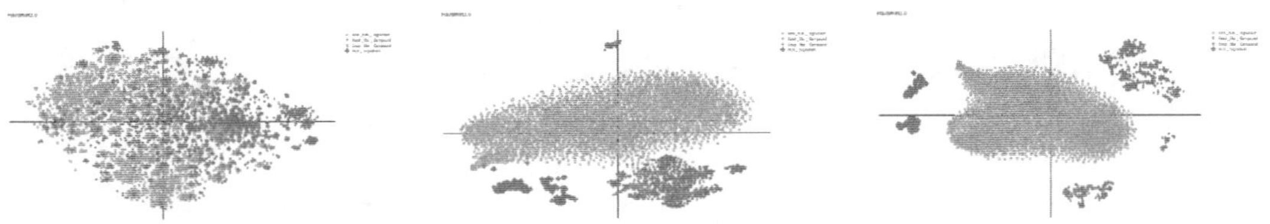

Figure 2: Embedding space comparison under different configurations, where each color represents a different category: **Yellow** (Non-hub Ingredient), **Green** (Food-like Compound), **Pink** (Drug-like Compound), and **Orange** (Hub Ingredient). (Left) Baseline embeddings show poor separation between ingredients and compounds. (Center) Flavor Diffusion (200 nodes) without CSP achieves improved clustering of chemical compounds and hub ingredients. (Right) Flavor Diffusion (200 nodes) with CSP results in well-defined clusters, leveraging chemical fingerprints to enhance separation.

effectively balances local (ingredient-level) and global (chemical-based) interactions, enhancing clustering quality and enabling meaningful extensions of ingredient networks.

7 Conclusion

This study presents FlavorDiffusion, a diffusion-based framework for predicting ingredient pairings and chemical interactions. By integrating chemical fingerprints and optimizing graph embeddings, the model enhances clustering quality and predictive accuracy. The CSP layer significantly improves food-chemical representations, achieving top NMI scores. The diffusion process enables generalization, inferring novel ingredient combinations. FlavorDiffusion aligns culinary and chemical properties, advancing flavor discovery with applications in computational gastronomy. Future work will expand datasets, integrate multi-modal data, and refine graph-sampling techniques to further food science research.

References

Garima Gupta and Rahul Katarya, "A Computational Approach Towards Food-Wine Recommendations", *Expert Systems With Applications*, vol. 238, p. 121766, 2024. doi:10.1016/j.eswa.2023.121766.

Javier Marín, Aritro Biswas, Ferda Ofli, Nicholas Hynes, Amaia Salvador, Yusuf Aytar, Ingmar Weber, and Antonio Torralba, "Recipe1M+: A Dataset for Learning Cross-Modal Embeddings for Cooking Recipes and Food Images", *IEEE Transactions on Pattern Analysis and Machine Intelligence*, 2019. doi:10.1109/TPAMI.2019.2908359.

Zuzanna Gawrysiak, Agata Żywot, and Agnieszka Ławrynowicz, "WineGraph: A Graph Representation For Food-Wine Pairing", *Advances in Neural Information Processing Systems (NeurIPS)*, 2023.

Rogério Xavier de Azambuja, A. Jorge Morais, and Vítor Filipe, "X-Wines: A Wine Dataset for Recommender Systems and Machine Learning", *Big Data Cogn. Comput.*, vol. 7, no. 20, 2023. doi:10.3390/bdcc7010020.

Bryan Perozzi, Rami Al-Rfou, and Steven Skiena, "DeepWalk: Online Learning of Social Representations", *Proceedings of the 20th ACM SIGKDD International Conference on Knowledge Discovery and Data Mining (KDD'14)*, 2014. doi:10.1145/2623330.2623732.

Zhiqing Sun and Yiming Yang, "DIFUSCO: Graph-based Diffusion Solvers for Combinatorial Optimization", *Neural Information Processing Systems (NeurIPS)*, 2023. doi:10.48550/arXiv.2302.08224.

Jiaming Song, Chenlin Meng, and Stefano Ermon, "Denoising Diffusion Implicit Models", *International Conference on Learning Representations (ICLR)*, 2021. doi:10.48550/arXiv.2010.02502.

Jonathan Ho, Ajay Jain, and Pieter Abbeel, "Denoising Diffusion Probabilistic Models", *Neural Information Processing Systems (NeurIPS)*, 2020. doi:10.48550/arXiv.2006.11239.

Yuxiao Dong, Nitesh V. Chawla, and Ananthram Swami, "metapath2vec: Scalable Representation Learning for Heterogeneous Networks", *Proceedings of the 23rd ACM SIGKDD International Conference on Knowledge Discovery and Data Mining (KDD'17)*, 2017. doi:10.1145/3097983.3098036.

Donghyeon Park, Keonwoo Kim, Seoyoon Kim, Michael Spranger, and Jaewoo Kang, "FlavorGraph: a large-scale food-chemical graph for generating food representations and recommending food pairings", *Scientific Reports*, vol. 11, p. 931, 2021. doi:10.1038/s41598-020-79422-8.

Author Index